Reconstructing Meaningful Life Worlds

A New Approach to Social Work Practice

Yumi Oshita, PhD,
and
Kiyoshi Kamo, MSW

iUniverse, Inc.
Bloomington

Reconstructing Meaningful Life Worlds
A New Approach to Social Work Practice

iUniverse books may be ordered through booksellers or by contacting:

iUniverse
1663 Liberty Drive
Bloomington, IN 47403
www.iuniverse.com
1-800-Authors (1-800-288-4677)

ISBN: 978-1-4620-0617-5 (sc)
ISBN: 978-1-4620-0616-8 (hc)
ISBN: 978-1-4620-0615-1 (ebk)

Library of Congress Control Number: 2011904380

Printed in the United States of America

iUniverse rev. date: 09/23/2011

CONTENTS

FOREWORD

I am delighted to be able to write on behalf of *Reconstructing Meaningful Life Worlds*, by Yumi Oshita, PhD & Kiyoshi Kamo, MSW, in Japan. Dr. Oshita was an eager student of mine of family therapy in the graduate program at Fukuoka University of Education. Together we developed the Clay Sculpture Technique and Family Image Technique (FIT) which represents a new approach to family therapy. Dr. Oshita also courageously conducted a cross cultural study which compares the power structure of the families of China and Japan with FIT.

In conjunction with Prof. Kamo, Dr. Oshita began joint research to further develop social work theory so as to be able to explain the dynamics of family interaction, as well as the development of corresponding clinical techniques to use in the client's ecological situation. *Reconstructing Meaningful Life Worlds* is the fruitful product of their thoughtful research in social work theory and methodology. It will stimulate and inspire others in the field looking for a new and creative approach to social work practice.

Kenji Kameguchi, PhD, Professor, The University of Tokyo
President, International Academy of Family Psychology

PREFACE

ESCAPE FROM THE STAGNATION
OF THEORY AND PRACTICE
IN SOCIAL WORK TODAY

Social work is roughly defined as the theoretical and practical system to intervene in mal-adaptive eco-systems, with the aim to improve the client's adaptation level. However, what really is social work theory? Furthermore, what is social work practice? If one browses through the journals of social work in Japan one will be disappointed, because the concept of the eco-system is obscure and skills are not clearly defined in these journals. To our regret, the theoretical level of the discussion about social work in these journals is basically no different from the guide book of the welfare administration of the Japanese central and local government.

To provide a method aimed at clearing the stagnation of theory and practice of social work, we have published many books in Japanese on social work theory and practice, written in Japanese. In these writings, we presented the direction of the theorization, developing skills, and measurement of the intervention effect from the point of view of social constructionism. However, there were few social workers who understood these discussions in Japan, except for some social workers in the Hiroshima social work research group who were up-to-date with these theories.

The main aim of this particular work is to provide social workers with a method to escape from their theoretical straight jackets and practice bottlenecks. How can the social worker be liberated from their theoretical cages?

The first precondition to escape from the cage is to have a suitable social theory that can be used to assess the structure of the interconnectedness and transformations of the social system. Grand social theory, for example structural-functional social systems theory (Parsons, 1951) is not useful to give the micro level analysis of social life situations where rules of action and recognition arise. What we need is a social theory that has the explanatory power for the fundamental transactional situation in which social systems emerge. We chose CMM (Coordinated Management of Meaning) (Cronen and Pearce, 1985, Cronen, Pearce, and Tomm, 1985, Pearce, 1994, 2007) as the basic theory to analyze the micro, meso, and macro levels of the eco system. On one hand, CMM is a theory to help comprehend the dynamics of the occurrence of the meaning, as well as behavioral rules in transactions. On the other hand, it theorizes the dynamics of the over-determined structure of the social system. A problematic situation is defined as the maladaptive over-determined structure in which a pseudo-solution activity continues according to these rules. These behavioral and meaning construction rules operate as the context to select future new behavior, and the new behavior transforms the old rules. If we can change these problem maintenance rules, we can change the problem amplifying behaviors, and vice versa. As a social system consists of interconnected subsystems of these rules, minimum change of one subsystem expands to changing other systems. Consequently, the equilibrium of the entire problematic eco-system collapses. Moreover, the power of this theory for problem solving is seen in the intervention activities. In the following chapters, a social theory of social work based on this CMM theory is shown.

Although CMM's explanation of meaning construction mechanism is very creative and its logic of explanation is precise, its explanation of behavior rule is much vaguer and imprecise than is the explanation of meaning construction mechanisms. Therefore we refined our act selection theory and added this theory to create a more holistic meaning construction theory. What is wholly original in our approach is a theoretical framework for social work practice which explains speech acts not only from the viewpoint of the receiver's meaning construction, but from the point of view of the sender's utterance selection. Our approach here also includes a new transformation and measurement theoretical framework. The resulting new theoretical model is a modified version of CMM (MCMM). The method of the problem solution is derived from MCMM theory as discussed below.

The second precondition of the new social work is to have clearly defined an effective problem solving skills set. Our discussion of problem solving skills starts from the definition of the problem. The problem of the client is not considered to be an objective entity. We define the problem as the system of the explanation constructed by the client through a range of transactions. Based on this social constructionist definition of the problem, we adopt client interviewing skills that reconstitute the amplified complaint of the problem according to a time series. Each of the elements in the transaction is changed as a result of the application of this special problem-solving method. These are the systems of mixed skills which consist of the skills of the circular questions and the skills of the solution focused approach. We have abandoned the traditional problem solving method of social work which searches for the invisible ultimate cause of the problem occurrence and tries to remove it. Examples of the use of our techniques are shown in the following chapters.

In addition, a systematized methodology to measure the intervention effect is presented as the third precondition of this new social work practice. Our method to measure the intervention effect is original. This measuring methodology is based on the perspective of social constructionism. It not only quantitatively compares the incidence of each of the elements of the transaction between pre- and post-interventions, but also represents a method for comparing the difference of the dynamism of reality construction between these interventions.

Personal History

This book presents a system of new theory and skills of social work based on social constructionist perspective which is not available in any academic journals in Japan at this time. We, the writers of this book, are teachers at a small provincial prefectural university in western Japan (Hiroshima).

For Prof. Kamo, his history of research and practice in social work started from 1970. He was employed by the hospital for autistic children as the social worker because he had psychoanalytic intervention skills. His first academic research about social work was concerned with the intervention for autistic children and their families, based on psychoanalytic theory. There were a lot of theorists who tried to explain the appearance of the autistic syndrome using object relations theory, but this psychoanalytic approach could not show any real positive therapeutic results.

On the other hand, structuralism was advocated as a basic theory of the behavioral science as a kind of counter at that time. Prof. Kamo designed a support model for the family of the autistic child. It was aimed at intervention in the transaction between parents and their children in daily life situations based on Piaget's structuralist developmental theory. This Piagetian intervention model for the family of the autistic child has been proven to be effective through many social work practices. He obtained new knowledge not only about skills to change the behaviors of autistic children, but also skills to transform problematic family relationships.

However, as the main focus of intervention of this model was the relation between a mother and a autistic child, its ability to transform a whole family and its background system were low.

In the 1980's Prof. Kamo shifted the object of the research from autism to family relationships. Structural family therapy encouraged his clinical research of the family, because he was strongly influenced by structuralism at that time.

Family centered social work practice model influenced by the knowledge of structural family therapy appeared in the 1980's. Hartman and Laird's social work practice models showed the system of the assessment and transformation skills of the life situation based on this structural family therapy. The concept of structure used there was not strictly defined and skills had not been integrated. However they were the precursors who showed the structural social work model which defined a family and its background system as a structure.

Prof. Kamo introduced the eco-map which was a basic tool for assessment; he refined the transformation technique and published his work in a domestic academic journal in the 1980's. However, even this eco-map approach was not accepted by domestic social workers until the early 21st century. Moreover, social workers in Japan have little knowledge about transformation techniques which Hartman and Laird now provide.

Structuralist language theory became the popular scientific paradigm in 1980s. The narrative model of White (who was a social worker and a family therapist) emerged from this philosophical background. Hartman and Laird understood this model as an original postmodern model of family therapy and social work practice. They proposed a conversion of theory into the narrative model from their previous modern family-centered social work practice model.

Institutionalized level of story and the level of the speech act were connected directly without putting parameters in his clinical theory. The research that proved the effectiveness of practicing of this model was missing, though it had been actively advocated from the 1990's to the early 21st century in Japan.

Prof. Kamo's concern at this time was to correct White's deterministic narrative model, and to restructure it to more useful clinical practice model.

It was the concept of a difference that he integrated in the new body of practice theory. The concept of difference was widespread in France and the United States, as the key concept to reconstruct the old epistemology and ontology in the 80's. Fortunately, he found that the concept of this difference was used as the basic theory of clinical practice at Calgary University in Canada. The systemic approach of Karl Tomm based on the concept of difference was more impressive than structural family therapy. This approach showed a sophisticated concept of the family. It defined the family as a system in which difference flows circularly between family members and between embedded levels meaning structure of a person. Based on this refined post modernistic definition of a system, Tomm designed very useful clinical skills named as the circular questions which are used to activate the emergence of differences in the family system. In the 1990s he practiced these skills to solve problems of many clients and confirmed its usefulness.

Prof. Kamo tried to restructure the narrative model which lacked the ability to transform a maladaptive process in ecological situations based on the theory of the activation of difference, and clinical skills of circular questions. He published several books which showed the new body of the theory and skills of social constructionist social work in the early 21st century, however, these writings were unexpectedly criticized by many researchers and practitioners of social work. They criticized the method and the theoretical orientation as a kind of pedantry.

To our regret it is not easy to continue an academic discussion about the new theory construction of social work practice in Japan.

Prof. Oshita's story begins from the end of 1980 when she met her teacher at Hiroshima Women's University; that teacher was Professor Kamo who is a co-author of this book. She was very interested in systems theory, social constructionism and family therapy which he taught. The concept that social reality is constructed by language especially captivated her. Afterward, she entered in the graduate school of Fukuoka University of Education and studied family therapy. Prof. Kenji Kameguchi was the advisor of her research. He was famous for his translation of '*Foundations of family therapy: a conceptual framework for systems change*' which was written by Lynn Hoffman (1981). She acquired a new practical perspective for analyzing the change in family system through his guidance.

He used unique techniques which focused on human perception in family counseling. One of the techniques was the Clay Sculpture Technique. The creation of a Clay Sculpture Technique was a non-verbal method to decrease the tension of client and his or her family, and it was used to activate the interaction between participants in the session, too. Although she could assess the positive changing process of the clients by analyzing the dynamics of the participants' transference of their conflict into the sculpture, its ability to explain the changing mechanism of total family was weak.

On the other hand, while studying the effectiveness of the Clay Sculpture Technique, She joined a volunteer group in Fukuoka which offered the program of group therapy to children who had the syndrome of *school refusal* or psychosomatic illness. These children who participated in this therapeutic program, had to attend the camp program for almost a week at the Tian Shan in Shinjang Uyghur Autonomous Region of China. They had to find new adaptive behaviors in a new and different cultural context which they had never experienced, namely they had to abandon their old defensive skills of withdrawing from their uneasy human relationships. Some children and their parents could radically transform their original pathological behavior selection rules and meaning construction rules after participating in this program. This group therapy which intervenes in the macro context of the children's and their families' life situation had the power to radically change their adaptation level. Ms. Oshita was impressed by the force of cultural context to change a person's behavior and cognition.

However, both these methods were very artificial. Some of the children who had improved their pathological behavior in Uyghur deteriorated their adaptation when they returned to Japan. This data motivated Ms. Oshita to create a new therapeutic method to intervene in a person's ecological life situation.

After finishing the program of graduate school, Ms. Oshita took part in the project of grants-in-aid for scientific research with Professor Kenji Kameguchi. This research was a cross cultural comparison study which compared the power structure of the families of Uyghur and Japan for three years. At that time she did research comparing the image of the family structure of junior high school students who lived in China and Japan by using Family Image Technique (FIT). The FIT was an effective tool to analyze the power structure of the Han people's family system in urban China.

However, this model did not have enough power to explain the power structure of the Uyghur family who lived in the rural Shinjang Uyghur Autonomous Region of China, because of the dynamics of transactions and its structure of their families were too complex to be analyzed by FIT. This experience of field research changed Ms. Oshita's family research method. After this experience of this research, she reached the conclusion that what was needed was not a research model which uses existing test batteries, but a model to investigate the family's reality construction process directly and intensively in the ecological life situation.

Prof. Kamo and Ms. Oshita's joint research began from 2000 when Ms. Oshita came back in order to study under Prof. Kamo at Hiroshima Prefectural Women's University. This was the beginning of the second stage of research and practice for her.

This stage was characterized as the stage of the development of practical theory and techniques. The theoretical foundation to explain the dynamics of the family interaction and the clinical techniques to use in the clients' ecological situation were refined under Professor Kamo.

Ms. Oshita was employed as the first social worker at the Hiroshima University Hospital in 2001. The main practice in this hospital was to help the patients' social adjustment, and establish teams between various medical staff. Clients of her social work practice were HIV/AIDS patients and patients with psychosomatic illnesses. She defined their problem as the maladaptive transactions between their personal and physical context in their life situation in which the generation of a rule of new speech acts was being prevented. Many practices were tried in order to change these maladaptive situations by using circulating questions and the technique of Solution Focused Brief Therapy (SFBT).

In 2006, Ms. Oshita entered the doctoral course of the graduate school of Yamaguchi Prefectural University to systematize the clinical theory of social support network which can promote a person's health and welfare in the ecological life situation. She studied under Prof. Takeo Ogawa is a renowned professor for the study of community organizations for the health of elderly peoples. The results of her doctorial study was published as a book in 2010; "*Clinical Theory of Support Network.*" She also published a book in 2008 called, "*New Human Services Theory*"

In 2000, Oshita and Kamo organized the Hiroshima School of Social Work (HSSW) where we worked to deepen the understandings of theory and skills of circular questions, and SFBT. Moreover, we are currently doing social work at the following institutions, for example psychiatric settings, a child guidance clinic, a residential care institution for the children, University Hospital for HIV/AIDS patients and chronic pain patients.

This particular work in hand is intended to reach a broader audience for describing a new approach to social work theory and practice. Though it is the product of two (or more) Japanese social workers, the intervention practices and theoretical model on which it is based should have universal application.

The Construction of This Book

In PART 1, an outline for the new theory and skills is given. Chapter 1 deals with the consideration of these theory and techniques, and provides a new conceptualization for these key concepts. In Chapter 2, traditional moral theory in social work is critically examined and new perspectives for theorizing the supporting principles of social work are exemplified. Chapter 3 presents the system of new skills and outlines the new measurement methodology which is used.

Thus PART 1 sets out the theoretical considerations for the theory, provides a skills and measurement method, and then in PART 2, the effectiveness of the intervention model which was discussed in the PART 1 is examined through case studies. In Chapter 4 of PART 2, a social work practice to transform a client's story filled with suffering is discussed from a social constructionist standpoint. The client was a girl with hyperventilation who was a junior high school student living in a residential care institution for children. Her complaint of hyperventilation is assessed as the suffering story amplified in the communication process between nursing staff and herself. The intensive intervention process in the dynamics of her creation of suffering story using circular questions and solution focused skills was shown.

In Chapter 5 of PART 2, a new social constructionist community social work practice with a client who refused to leave the hospital is presented. The client had serious atopic dermatitis and complained of hypersensitivity of smell in her apartment. Her complaints of olfactory hypersensitivity were assessed as a defense of her basic interpersonal ontological insecurity which had originated in her family. It was proliferated in her interpersonal transaction in the hospital, in the agency of public case workers and the other systems in her life world. To change her defense, circular questions, positive reframing, and scaling questions were used. The resolution process of her interpersonal ontological insecurity and construction process of her new reality are intensively described.

In Chapter 6 of PART 2, a social work practice for the client who can't leave the hospital though she tried to is discussed. The intervention process in this case was more complex than the case described in Chapter 5. This intervention is composed of three phases as follows: At first, the client is helped to find the behavior to control her chronic pain of somatoform by circular questions which are the intervention skills to differentiate elements of problem amplifying process and change the dynamics of this process. Second, based on the acquisition of the new solution behavior and the definition of self as a person who has the ability to design a solution, she is helped to change the rules of her transactional language game played between her doctor and herself. As a result, the client succeeds in changing the prescription of the doctor and got permission to temporarily leave the hospital. Both the pre-intervention phase and the post-intervention phase are plotted on three-dimensional graphs and the difference of the dynamics between two phases is analyzed. Third, the generative dynamics of achievement of reinstatement is described through the process of using the skills of problem resolution to minimize the problem acquired by social worker's intervention in the language game.

Acknowledgement

The authors would like to deeply thank Dr. Steven L. Rosen. He patiently read our manuscripts and kindly pointed out many mistakes in our expressions and gave us useful advice. This work would not have been possible without his help.

Secondly, we would like to thank Emi Fujiwara, Kazushi Kawamoto, Tomoyo Nishida who are members of the Hiroshima School of Social Work (HSSW). We developed many of our ideas from our discussions with them. They gave us the opportunity to reflect on our theory.

Lastly, we want to express our gratitude for Api which is a wire fox terrier and for Nana which is a kuro shiba. When our work was slow in developing, their cheerfulness always encouraged us.

Kiyoshi Kamo
Yumi Oshita

PART 1

CHAPTER 1

OUTLINE FOR THE NEW SOCIAL WORK

KIYOSHI KAMO

Social Work Reconstructed

The most serious problem that exists in traditional social work practice is the absence of a systematized social theory. This basic problem goes beyond the level of systematization of theory to something deeper. Even the idea that the construction of a theoretical system is a necessary condition for understanding social phenomenon is not necessarily shared by social workers in Japan. Naturally, the absence of an adequate social theory results in the absence of a coherent social work methodology. Therefore, a second problem is the absence of an effective practice theory. Following this is the absence of a method to measure the effects of practice. The single case design has been a refined research method used in social work intervention (Theyer and Wodarski, 2007), however, this is a research model to measure behavioral change of the individual. This research model cannot measure the transactional process in life situations.

How can we then provide an adequate theory for social work practice? The answer to this question is not easy. The procedure for problem solving in the natural sciences is summarized as follows: the subject doing the observation objectively analyzes the mechanism of the generation of the problem, identifies the cause of the problem generation, and tries to remove it. This whole approach is epistemologically denied in the social constructionist approach. For starters, social constructionism denies the concept of the real existence of a 'problem'. Furthermore, it denies the possibility of objective observation; it is thus a kind of metaphysics. The idea of pure observation not influenced by outer conditions is actually metaphysical, because in the circuit of human communication the sender's message is processed and realized by the receiver, who punctuates the sequence of messages of the sender based on the context of his reality construction (Wilden, 1980, pp. 112-117). This theory asserts that the 'problem' is the unique construction of the life situation by the client (Gergen, 1985). This new theoretical frame transforms the 'problem' of the client by the solution focused method. Transforming the method of the problem construction of the client is the strategy for solving the 'problems' of the client of this theory. In this approach the authors of this book have shifted the philosophical basis of the practice from logical empiricism to a social constructionist perspective. In following chapters practice theory, practice technique, and the research method based on the social constructionist theory are discussed. We begin by asking the question, what is precisely social theory which is based on social constructionism?

Social Theory

Social Theory as the Precondition for the Social Work Practice

The object of social work intervention are human transactions where new social situations are continually being generated anew. Analyses of these transactions are impossible without using some theoretical framework. The social worker often drowns in a flood of information without this theoretical framework to help make sense of what transpires. It is necessary to reconstruct the client's discourse about the problem by using a theoretical framework for problem solving. The purpose of an analysis of a transaction in social work practice is to clarify the contradiction amplifying mechanisms in the social situation based on this new theoretical framework of problem solving. This theoretical framework should have the power to explain the amplification process of the case. Structural social theories that are often used to explain the transactional social process in social work are highly systematized theories. These grand theories translate the dynamics of the daily life situation into refined concepts of systems theory (Bertalanffy, 1968). These are overarching theories, however, and their power to prescribe a method to change the transaction process of daily life is weak. Theoretical reconsideration of systems theory to construct the practice theory, without falling into excessive abstraction, is required by the social worker. The specific problem imposed on us as theorists, is to construct a clinical systems theory that can adequately stand up to, and be effective for new practice.

Construction of a Clinical Social Systems Theory

According to systems theory, the concept of the social is defined as a human system which has a set of various elements which are interconnected. This aspect of interconnectedness of elements is the structure; continued interaction develops between elements. Therefore, the social is defined as the system which has both structure and process (Constantine, 1986, pp. 45-68). The whole of the relationship between elements in the system is the structure. For instance, a husband who is the elemental ingredient of the family system and a wife who is a basic constituent, mutually unite. This is the marital system. In addition, a unique transaction develops between the family system and outer systems. The structure between systems of this family and outside the family is called as the supra system. When the child is born, the parent and child subsystem is generated within the family system and the structure and process of the family system then changes.

By process, we mean the dynamics of the transactional movement of the system. The dynamics of the transaction between these elements is analyzed by using the concept of the feedback loop. This loop is composed of two loops which mutually perform different functions. One is the positive feedback loop that explains a circular deviance amplification process between elements, and the other is the negative feedback loop that decreases the deviance. The system constructs the moving stability by circular dynamics between these two loops. Usually small contradictions are generated in this balanced system. When this small contradiction cannot be solved, the deviance amplifies in the system. This is the positive feedback loop. The transformation of the deviance amplifying process begins by the differentiation of old solution behavior in the system. This differentiation expands in the system, and the balance of system becomes perturbed. This perturbation of the structure and the process in the system is the beginning of the second-order change (Watzlawick, Weakland and Fisch, 1974, pp. 77-91).

Concept of Difference and System Change

If we accept Bateson's definition of the system, the system is defined as a set of differences where information as the difference flows in a circular fashion (Tomm, 1985, p. 38). The system transformation begins when the difference in this system is activated. Actualization of difference triggers a change in the whole system. The purpose of analysis of the transaction is to clarify the contradiction amplifying mechanisms in the social situation based on this new theoretical framework. For instance, let's assume the transactional system consisted of A and B. At first A sends the message to B. A gives B visual stimulation, aural stimulation, and tactile stimulation. But the message of A is not a physical quantity for B. B processes this message as information that transmits difference, and constructs meaning from it. A similarly handles the message B sends. In a word, system process is defined as the circular process that generates differences. This dynamic cannot be analyzed by the linear causal relationship that considers physical power to be cause. When the structure and the process of this subsystem differentiate, this change influences the movements of other subsystems. As a result, the total system will change. A minor change of elements of the system produces entire system changes. This is the principle of intervention in the minimalist approach.

Social Network

The interconnectedness of subsystems forms the social network. The simple structure of a social network is represented in the Figure 1.1. (Hartman and Laird, 1983, Laird and Hartman, 1985).

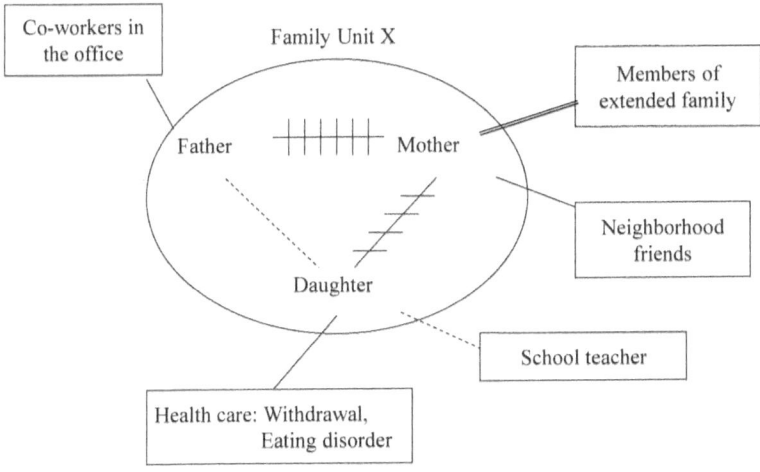

Figure 1.1. Network System of Family and Its Outer Organizations

The nature of the interconnectedness of family X and its outer systems is pictured using different lines (Laird, 1985, pp. 392-393)

This is a network system that has seven network subsystems. Each network subsystem functions according to the principle of maintaining homeostasis, or negative and positive feedback loops. Activating the transformation power of the subsystem of the network is the intervention strategy into the problem maintenance system.

For example, let's assume the first daughter has anorexia. If any of the subsystems is transformed, a force to change her behavior will be generated in this system. If the social worker changes the mal-adaptation processes of one or more network subsystems to a more adaptive position, the dynamics of groups of interconnected subsystems will also be transformed, and this girl's adaptation level may improve. The principle of the intervention to the network is to generate minute differences in the network subsystem. Let us take for example, the mother and the daughter subsystem as the target of the intervention. The change of mother's message or the differentiation of daughter's way of understanding her mother transforms the dynamics of this dyadic system. By effective professional intervention, the frequency of exchange of positive messages may increase. Furthermore, messages having the force to solve the problem might increase among two persons by this intervention. When the structure and the process of this subsystem change, this change influences the movements of other subsystems. Then the transformation of this network subsystem will expand to the transformation to the entire network system.

Embedded Levels of the Context of the Social Structure

Cronen and Pearce (1985, p. 72) define the social structure as the embedded levels of the context. These are represented as follows:

1. Speech acts: relational meanings of the person's messages.
2. Episodes: connected patterns of the speech act.
3. Relationships: subject's definition of the relationship of the two or more persons.

4. Life script: subject's definition of the self.
5. Family myth: abstract conception of the family, society.

A Modified Version of Coordinated Management of Meaning (CMM)

Original definitions of speech act emphasized the importance of the receiver's relational meaning construction of the sender's utterance. To this definition we incorporated the sender's relational meaning construction of his or her own message. Thus, we have a modified version of CMM, and we have named this new theoretical system: MCMM (modified CMM). The sender's relational meaning construction of his or her own utterance is shown as 's' and receiver's relational meaning construction of sender's utterance is shown as 'm'. Figure 1.4. in this chapter shows a practice model to transform deviance amplifying transactions based on this modified speech act theory of Coordinated Management of Meaning (MCMM). A concrete example of an intervention using this theoretical framework is shown in Figure 3.2., Figure 3.3., and Figure 3.4. in Chapter 3 we provide a coherent research model based on MCMM.

Each level functions as the context of the movement of other levels. For example, episodes of life events function as the context of the meaning construction of the actual utterance selection. The speech act level operates as the context for the construction of the new relationship. The mother's new selection of the message may change the daughter's definition of the relationship. Therefore this is a multilayered social system theory.

Mind and Matters

Of course, people cannot always be well adapted under very poor material conditions. Human transaction is also always embedded in particular material conditions. However, these conditions don't exist alone as a material in the process of the interaction. The physical world is the world personified by the subject of the transaction. For example, the taste of coffee for the couple who hates each other is greatly different from the taste of coffee of the loving couple. The bitterness of the relationship is the context that produces the bitterness of coffee, and the bitterness of coffee produces feedback into the bitterness of the relationship. A circular relationship exists between the personal elements and external environmental elements in the human communication. These material conditions influence the dynamics of the interpersonal relationship. At the same time the mind decides the meaning of the external world. Viewed from this perspective, linear explanations that presuppose a single one-way cause of the mal-adaptation are inadequate theories which fail to take into account the integrative nature of mind (Bateson, 1979). The necessary condition to analyze the mal-adaptation of a client is a detailed analysis of the dynamics between individual mind and material context.

Social Work as a Practice to Improve Problem Solving Skills

The Transformative Power of Micro-level Analysis

As said earlier, a human system is composed of interconnected subsystems. The minimum basic subsystem is an individual who constructs meanings of others' acts, then acts on the basis of this interpretation. This is where the intervention point of the social constructionist approach comes in. When the person's method of giving the meaning to the message and the way of act selection differentiate, this micro level change spreads to the entire macro system. If the theoretical frame to analyze the micro process of the meaning construction and the act selection is used, the accuracy of the systems analysis of daily life increases. MCMM that can explain the process of increasing deviance as a transactional process between micro, meso, and the macro levels is indeed, a useful theory for social work. MCMM explains a system transformation as follows: First of all, the difference in the meaning composition and the act selection is generated at the micro level. This minor change at the speech acts levels operates as the force to transform the other levels. For example, the daughter with an eating disorder says to her mother, "I do not like this bread". Mother abandons the usual critical attitude to the daughter and responds to her positively, saying that, "You can clearly insist on the flavor of the meal." Mother's positive reframing of the anorexic behavior of the daughter will become the context for change of the former daughter's definition of the relationship. In this transaction, the mother's minor change of behavior operates as the higher context for the daughter's acquisition of the new definition of the relationship. In the next meal scene, this new definition of the relationship will operate as the context for the selection of the new utterances of the daughter. That is, the minor change functions as the context for the change of the entire system. This is the epistemology of the system oriented social worker.

A Social Constructionist Approach to Solving the Client's Problems

Usually the complaint of the client can be expressed as follows: "I have desperately tried to solve problems. I have continued to ask for advice from others and have tried to change the situation. Still, my own problem has not been solved. What should I do?" Unfortunately, the more he or she tries to find a solution, the more the problem becomes amplified. This is the 'pseudo-solution' process which the client has produced (Watzlawick, Weakland and Fisch, 1974). The client amplifies a contradiction inherent in this process. Therefore, the problem of adaptation can be defined as a situation where the client perpetuates conflict in the interaction process. From the social constructionist perspective, the problem is not considered to be an actual discrete entity, but is defined as the socially constructed story by clients. Through the process of the pseudo solution, the client doesn't see the utterances and meaning construction that have power to solve the conflict. In other words, the social constructionist offers an entirely new definition of what constitutes a 'problem' and this new perspective opens up the possibility for deep resolution of client issues.

The purpose of social work is to increase the power of the problem solving of the client in a particular social system. Intervention skills that differentiate ways of act selection and meaning construction of the client are used to solve the problems. This is accomplished because social constructionist offers a deeper, more accurate understanding of how so-called "problems" are the result of transactions in meaningful contexts.

The Role of the Social Worker

The role of the social worker is to engage the transactions of the family and its outer system described by the client, and to differentiate these transactions which are perpetuating problems. Some logical-empirical social work theories strongly insist that the solution method is discovered if the problem is objectively observed (Hudson, 1978). That is, the perspective of traditional social work is based on first-order cybernetics (Keeney, 1983). Figure 1.2. indicates this first-order cybernetics. However, social workers cannot objectively observe the problematic transaction of the target system. The problem re-definition and the solution arise through the process of the transaction between a social worker and a client. It is impossible for a social worker to observe the client's life situation objectively and identify the ultimate cause of the amplification of the problem.

The first-order cybernetics model is the theoretical basis for analyzing the maladaptive transactional process. This epistemological framework of the social work practice gives the rationale to objectify the structure of the problem and identify the circular feedback mechanism of the target system to the social worker.

However, the logical ground of the basic assumption of practice which presupposes the objective observation of the problem amplifying mechanism (the mechanism of the first-order cybernetics) is unstable.

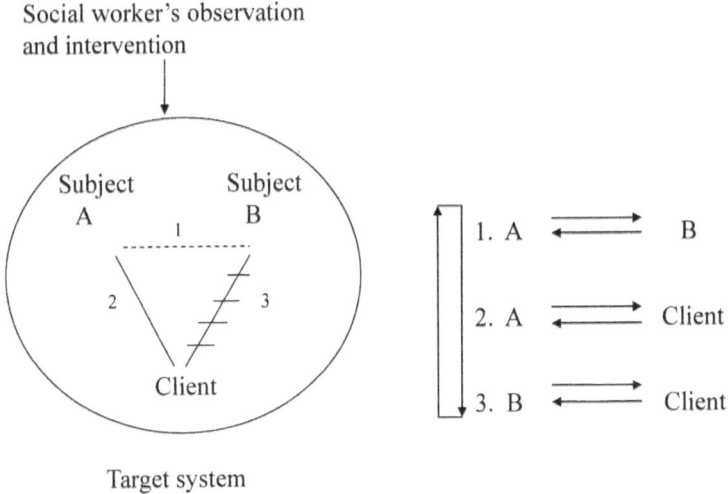

Target system

Figure 1.2. First-Order Cybernetics

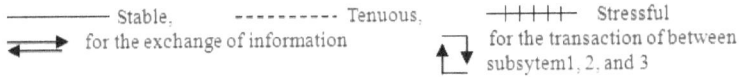

Usually the helping activity is done according to the following procedures. At first, the social worker who has the theoretical background of social constructionism encourages the client to explain the dynamics of his or her suffering human relationship. Second, this social worker chooses the sequence of the typical problematic transaction process as the target of the transformation and creates the map of the structuring process of the problem. As the problematic system of the client is composed of the interconnected group of transactions, transformation of one transaction spreads to the entire system change. Therefore the social worker can draw many kinds of assessment maps and choose the intervention target freely.

The way of the target selection is not fixed. The social worker does not seek after the ultimate cause that generates the problematic situation. He does not need the practice guideline which presupposes the ultimate cause and prescribes the object assessment. After the assessment, the social worker differentiates this deviant circular movement of these interconnected systems by using special intervention skills. The differentiation of the dysfunctional system operates as the context which reconstructs the social worker's original assessment. In this way, the social worker cannot isolate his or her observation from the transformation of the target system. The social worker has to relate to the interconnected problematic transactions system and assess the dynamics of the target system. Moreover, he or she has to observe the transaction process between the target system and his or her intervention. The data can be conceptualized as a kind of input which is drawn out from this changing process in the practice method and modifies the former assessment and intervention. That is, the social worker relates to the co-generating of two kinds of cybernetic systems. As Figure 1.2. shows, the social worker relates to the dynamics of the client's deviant system as the target ('first-order cybernetics'). At the same time, the social worker relates to the circular transaction between the target system and his or her practice (cybernetics of cybernetics). This theory of 'second-order cybernetics' (Keeney, 1983) has the high compatibility with social constructionism (Figure 1.3.). Second-order cybernetics is the basic theoretical framework that explains the co-generating mechanism of the solution activities between the social worker and the client.

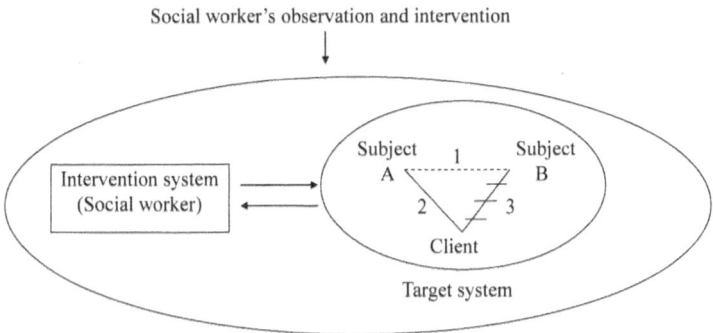

Figure 1.3. Structure of 'Second-Order Cybernetics' in Social Work Practice

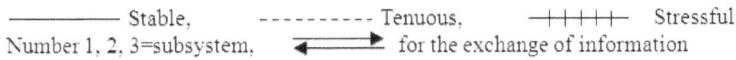

——————— Stable,   - - - - - - - - - Tenuous,   —+++++— Stressful
Number 1, 2, 3=subsystem,   ◄═══► for the exchange of information

Tracking Data and Problem Solution Skill

A client can identify his or her deviance amplifying sequence by tracking; the sequence of the problem story of the client is converted into the data of the sequence of the utterance and meaning construction by descriptive circular questions (DCQ) of the social worker (Figure 1.4.). Descriptive circular questions are intervention skills designed to elicit information to trigger the change (Tomm, 1985, p. 35). This speech act level is reciprocally related to the levels of the more abstract context as explained in the above-mentioned 'embedded levels of the context of the social structure'. The social worker helps the client describe the relations between those contexts and identify the pre-figurative force that influences the act selection and the meaning construction.

A (Mother)

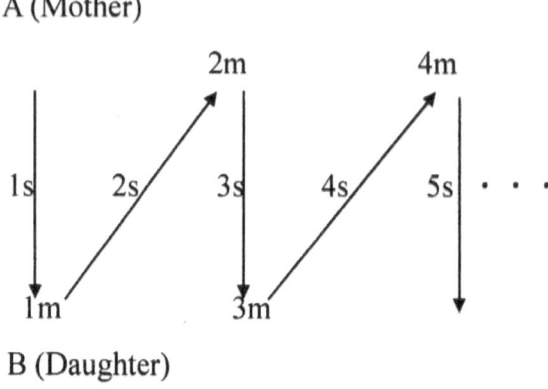

B (Daughter)

Figure 1.4. Tracking Data of Dyad System

Subject A and subject B are members of dyad transaction system. The sequence starts from A-1s. The sequence of actions is represented by 1s-5s. 1m-4m shows the sequence of the meaning construction. For example,

1s (Mother's message): 'Eat the salad' → 1m (Daughter's meaning): Mother is too oppressive

The theoretical frame that explains the problem as the interconnectedness of the minimum element minimizes the problem. This minimization clarifies the intervention point.

The material conditions have an important role in the sequence of this interaction.

For instance,

1. If mother forces meals on the daughter with an eating disorder (episode level context).
2. The daughter assigns food the meaning of compulsion for mother (meaning, speech act level).
3. Then she rejects the meal (behavior, speech act level).

In this case, for the daughter, feeding herself means putting the mother's hostility in the inside of her body. The mother, however, understands food as being the nutrients necessary to maintain the daughter's body. These contradictory meaning systems of the meals amplify the deviance of this dyad system. Refusal of feeding is not the root problem in this case. The problem is the amplification of the contradiction of definitions of food between the mother and her daughter. The meaning of food of the daughter changes, if the transaction changes (speech act level context). The strategy of the problem solving here is the transformation of the dynamics of two feedback loops between mother and daughter, and between the person and the thing (food). In this case, the transformation of the meaning of the food changes the meaning relationship of the two persons. A proverb in Japan also expresses the above-mentioned two feedback loop well, saying that, "If you hate the priest (relation level context), you'll also hate even the frock that he wears." The problem in this situation is not the frock, but the dynamics of the crossed feedback loops of the information exchange between the priest and yourself, and between his frock and yourself.

Reflections on the Described Data and the Measurement of the Intervention

Reflexive circular questions (RCQ) form the skills needed to differentiate the elements of the tracking sequence described by the client which can trigger a whole system change. These questions encourage the client to reflect and differentiate their described tracking data of the sequence of utterances and meaning construction. This question method encourages the client to reflect on the reciprocal dynamics of their levels of embedded contexts (Tomm, 1985). At the same time, differentiation of the elements of the transaction is amplified by skills of a solution focused approach (Corcoran, 2003, pp. 56-80, Nelson and Thomas, 2007 and Connie and Metcalf, 2009). These include the miracle questions, scaling questions, and other solution focused changing skills. By using this circular questions and skills of the solution focused approach which attempts to generate differences in the transaction, the client acquires the new problem solving skills. As a result, the deviance amplifying feedback loops of the family and its background system become perturbed. If social workers have the theoretical framework to compare the phases of the described sequence, and the phases of the sequence of reflection, they can measure the intervention effect. This research framework to measure the intervention effect is described in the following chapters. Descriptive and reflexive circular questions based on CMM are intervention skills which analyze the meaning construction process and aim at a creation of new meanings. We show anew practice framework to transform both of a meaning construction and behavior selection by modifying this original question method in PART 2.

The Subject I and the Constructed World

The presupposition of an existence of a situation that is a priori to the use of language cannot be denied. To comprehend the primitive existential situation, a subject needs language. Without obeying the rules of the language system which is composed of syntax and semantics, the world cannot be constructed. Is the world image really a social construction conforming to those rules? According to the formal logic and rules of semantics, people believe they practice communication and they construct a particular life world. This is communication practice obeying institutionalized communication rules according to formal logic.

Social constructionist theory defines the "problem" as the socially constructed story by clients. This story-making of the world not only follows the above-mentioned institutionalized social rules but also this story-making is composed according to the particular world construction rules of the client. For example, family members' problem explanations and methods for the solution often conflict respectively. The decision as to the "correctness" of the explanation is difficult to make. Although each client transforms the primitive life situation obeying institutionalized formal rules, the world construction is impossible without the existence of the private pragmatic rules, as well. The existential *apriori* subject that performs this practice of the world construction is defined as *I* which is the fundamental precondition to explain our world production epistemologically and ontologically. Of course, the subject *I* cannot compose the world by isolating oneself from the world. The subject *I* both creates and internalizes the rules for the act selection and the rules for the definition of the situation through repeated transactions. The former are the rules of the world creation, and the latter are the rules which define the world. Rules for the behavior selection and for situation definition, function as the context of new practice of the world creation by subjects.

Two kinds of circularity can be identified in these transactional processes. One is the circular transaction between the subjects of the transaction who create the world. The other is the circular process between the context created in the process of the transaction and the actual utterance. Thus, the world is defined not as a static given, but rather as the result of a dynamic interplay which emerges in and by human transaction.

A Proposal for the Social Constructionist Social Worker

The urgent problem for social work practice is the composition of an adequate social theory with intervention skills. To our regret, traditional social work theory and skills are far from systematized. Our small hope is that theory and skills of social constructionist social work will operate as a new framework to differentiate traditional social work practice. We hope that more vigorous discussion and debate over the theory and practice spreads throughout the community of social workers.

CHAPTER 2

A New Perspective on Helping Principles

Fumie Yamagishi *

Introduction

It has been the basic theory of social work to respect without reservation, the self of the client, while in practice it often drives the social worker into a maze. To utilize the concept of the self in a more fertile way, we will propose a new stance for the "I" (noted as *I* in this chapter from here on). This concept can be used for constructing helping skills for social work practice from a pragmatic point of view.

Sequential citations of *The Casework Relationship* written by Biestek in 1950's textbooks reveal that, at present, certain basic principles have become orthodoxy in social work practice in Japan, especially from a theoretical point of view. Except for a few scholars whose major is in social work theory, these principles are accepted without criticism by most social workers here in Japan. Due to the

* Fumie Yamagishi is a licensed social worker at a correctional institution.

lack of the understanding as to how to recognize the subjective self, these principles inevitably have involved basic theoretical problems such as an inability to account for contingencies or dilemmas which don't neatly fit into the theoretical model. As a result, those principles superficially survive, without offering real critical skills to change the problems of clients.

In this article, subjective self and *I* are discussed to serve as the theoretical basis of social work practices, oriented forwards suggesting a practical frame for a communicational process with clients.

I and the Rules of Constitution and Regulation

I and Social Work Practices

The process of acquiring the I.

The constitution of an *I* appears in the process of the transaction between mothers and children during the infant stage of development. It arises in daily life conversation where we acquire the definition of another's point of view into that of an *I* beyond the ordinary occurrences of themselves at the empirical level. For example, a mother asks her son whose name is T, "T, is the egg yummy?", and he replies "Ya, yummy." The skillful mother talks to him, saying "Ya, T's egg is yummy," to reiterate his experience and to fix it into a certain style, unconsciously obeying the ordinary grammatical rules with the subject and verb. Through these daily conversations between persons, it is possible to establish *I* as a fundamental concept to relate oneself to the empirical world, and to constitute it for oneself. It is the *I* which provides a way to divide the world between the metaphysical level and empirical level (Refer to the arrow from *I* as Subject to World as Object shown in Figure 2.1.).

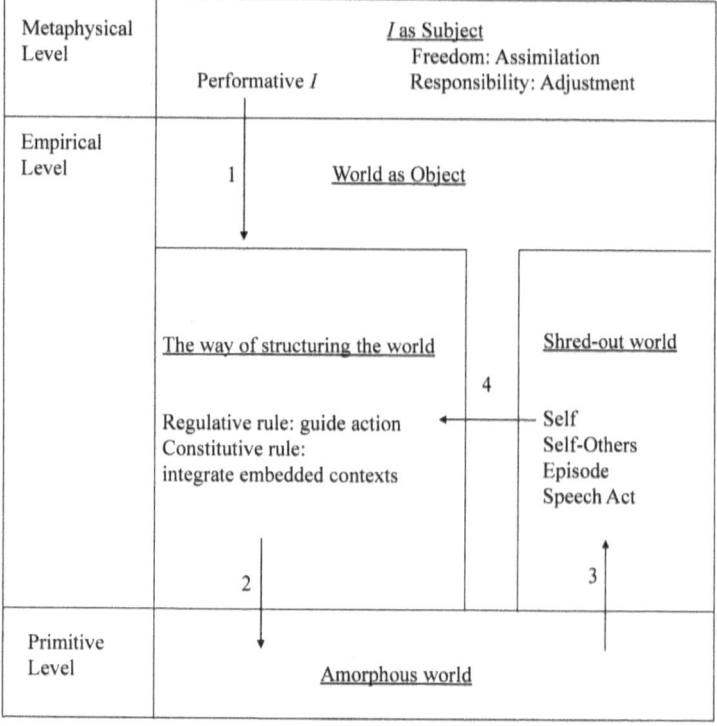

Figure 2.1. The Dynamics of *I* World Construction

The mother may then continue the conversation to say, "I prefer cabbages to eggs." This might open up the another form of dialogue with an implied point of view, even though the egg as object is the same; it will further deepen the understanding of the subject-object relationship. Certainly *I* is not pre-existent but rather an assumption, producing a statement with each phase as if it really existed. When one uses *I* in a way such as, "I watch, I listen, I move etc.", the partner in the dialogue also takes the expression of *I* for granted, as the first person in the grammatical system, even though what it implied is only the part of a body-mind gestalt being activated. As we set accustomed to using *I*, we are successful in placing *I* in a position that is free from the restriction of time and space to unite the objects of the empirical world and to construct a prototype of one's own world. At the same time it is also learned that each person has plural aspects of *I* which constitute a world of its own.

I *as the ruler of constitution and regulation.*

To utilize the concept of *I* as the grammatical first order in a social work practice which is aimed at respecting the client's self, an effective frame to deal with the client's reality is suggested in Figure 2.1. When people constitute the world as an object at the empirical level using *I,* freedom and responsibility must be taken into account as the foundation to support the subjectivity of *I.*

Freedom here means that in communicational process, where an infinite set of variables is always being produced, *I* lets everyone have their own way in constructing the world of self by setting the conceptual boundaries and selecting sentences to articulate and give them shape. Responsibility and adjustment here are two sides of the same coin, in the sense that the sentence expressed by *I* is practiced only by adjusting the self in response to the content involved. When *I* is used with a verb in a sentence, and it is the appearance of the performative *I,* it opens possibilities to attend to the world of objects at the empirical level in producing a world of meaning by the successive accumulations of actions, even though *I* itself still remains at the metaphysical level (1 in Figure 2.1.).

In this frame *I* is conceptualized in terms of private logic, because we believe that in daily language practices, which mainly deal with relationships, the client intends to raise the adaptation level with persons within his or her particular circumstances, rather than to break the discourse with which they are enclosed. Anderson noted that, "The *I* does not exist outside language, outside discourse; it is created and maintained in language and in discourse . . . . In other words, it is in and through language that a person constructs a personal account of the self" (1997, p. 219). We are inevitably engaged in language and discourse within which we have to manage to find a way to proceed; helping practices with *I* must focus on the process of meaning construction, not on external social rules such as public discourse, but rather on internal private rules of the client's unique case.

The way of structuring the world is understood based on the Coordinated Management of Meaning (CMM) theory, which is sometimes referred to as a rule-based approach for persons to structure their social reality; Regulative rules guide action and Constitutive rules integrate embedded contexts (Cronen, Pearce and Tomm, 1985). Sequential expressions of behavior or speculation based on these rules to an amorphous world at the primitive level are also repeatedly incorporated into rules, thus stabilizing the whole *I* world in a dynamic circular manner including two axes, one is subject-object and the other is freedom-responsibility (see arrows in Figure 2.1.). Thus *I* given freedom and responsibility, which is an abstract reality, can nevertheless function as a performative *I* in combination with a verb to activate the world as an object at the empirical level by the transmitting meaning of the client's inner world. It is in this inner world where Regulative rules and Constitutive rules are always manifesting as a deontic operator.

Elements in the amorphous world at the primitive levels are so infinite that they have the potential for the *I* to re-construct another reality. On the other hand, it is always the case in daily life that even small elements of an amorphous world appear in the empirical level as named objects according to the rules sustained by *I;* the whole process might be called jumping in the dark, where nobody could explore the amorphous world without light, without rules (2 in Figure 2.1.). Rules not only facilitate *I* in making decisions instantly, but also confine *I* to a restraining state, in contrast with the amorphous world of full rich originally.

Groups of elements are shred-out according to rules from an amorphous world (2 and 3 in Figure 2.1.) and function as a text, which also defines self, self-others, episodes and speech acts, all of which relate to each other in a circular manner. Since these texts are bundled into particular contexts, which is reflected again in the re-production of rules themselves (4 in Figure 2.1.), the world as object becomes in one sense stable and comfortable, yet in another sense rigid and conservative. Thus it must be noted that responsibility and freedom in a closed *I* system could paradoxically operate to threaten the *I* into certain restrictions in daily communication which might bring about mal-adaptation as a result. Even in that case, freedom and responsibility of the *I* are worth pursuing further because the worst solution is to abandon the *I* to the reality construction of the another person throughout, without activating the performative *I*.

Some explanation is also added to help understanding concepts in Figure 2.1. *I* is a metaphysical assumption and the amorphous world at the primitive level is also not real in that it does not appear as groups of elements to function without being shred-out. By analyzing the physics of producing various worlds which consist of *I* worlds as a whole in this manner, the world itself is revealed to be merely a process, within which the existence of heterogeneous levels is expanding, while keeping mutual relations. To deal with this continuous process of producing the world, utilization of an *I* which is assumed to be real, locating it in a positive position with freedom and responsibility, are effective. From this standpoint, the social worker as a counterpart of dialogue must not easily render the subjective constitution of the *I* to the world of true or false judgment according formal logic, just because the profession is premised upon making full use of the subjectivity of an *I*. Furthermore, it must be noted that only when people try to regulate actions and try to construct meaning on their own throughout each life scene, de-construction of such life world will also be possible on their own accord within the *I* world of pragmatic assumptions.

I *as subject of response-ability to others*

I as the subject of response-ability to others is derived from using that *I* to report the ideas which inevitably maintain a pragmatic commitment to oneself. In the communication process, setting *I* at the responsible position for the constitution and regulation of reality makes it possible to elicit messages from others. According to the reaction of the others, *I* continues to respond positively by choosing constitution and regulation freely in terms of response-ability. Second order "You" (it is the *I* on the side of you) as another counterpart to whom the message is reflected in and with each other, is essentially needed to establish *I*, producing a specific world between the actors. These processes are indicated in Figure 2.2.

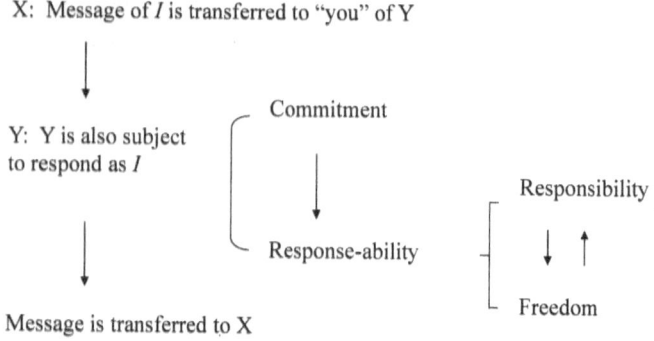

Figure 2.2. Dynamic Processes of World Construction between X and Y

"I have pain in my head" which is treated as if the pain existed in reality, is judged from empirical standards such as body temperature. The professional identity of medical staff to treat the symptoms is derived from objective and scientific manipulation standing on the logic of cause and effect. But in these practices, where the message of "I have headache" is only assigned to a numerical value of body temperature, no human relationship is available between *I*, "You" and "He" or "She" as individuals. On the other hand, how can social workers as professions of human relations approach this situation? Alternatively, they may try to approach the client in terms of response-ability and ask him or her to re-describe the pain, expressing his or her context in which the message of "pain" including non-linguistic meaning is articulated.

In this practice, even if the client with 37 degrees of body temperature strongly complains, Constitutive rules and Regulative rules which are reflected in the construction of the specific world of *I* might be revealed by the re-description of his or her situation. This is the first step to approach the *I*-world of meaning in terms of systematic relationships. At first, a certain sequence of exchanging messages with each other exists, and it can acquire a secondary place of existence in various ways by being re-examined and defined in the co-operating process of tracking the sequence again with the other person in the social worker role. Through these practices, reality is assumed not to be a set of static objects in existence, but the result of subjective engagement in a process of reality construction between any persons. Thus, clients' descriptions to explain their problems according to their own logic must not be evaluated in terms of true or false logic; in daily life, Constitutive rules and Regulative rules of clients are very complicated and interrelated in a circular manner as Bateson describes; it would be highly superficial as social worker to give the names of a symptom or to extract several rules which seemed to be ostensible objective reasons. Rather, to take a moral stance for the clients in social work practice, a social worker is not there just to accept what the client passively says, but rather tries to engage positively as a counterpart, joining the process of producing another specific context to construct an *I*.

It must be noted that establishing an alternative story to help clients to become liberated from discourse using the narrative approach (White and Epston, 1990) is different from what we are aiming at here, because in our practice the *I* is activated to commit the private transaction more intensively to promote response-ability as subject, and a solution story is situated in the same extension of *I*'s procedure, in *I*'s logical consistency without adding extra indefinable discourse.

Yumi Oshita, PhD, and Kiyoshi Kamo, MSW

Reconsideration of Biestek's Principles

Subject of Biestek's Social Work Practice in Relation to Seven Principles

Biestek indicated seven principles to actualize relationships with clients in his "Casework Relation" in 1957. They are as follows, Individualization, Purposeful expression of feelings, Controlled emotional involvement, Acceptance, The non-judgmental attitude, Client self-determination and Confidentiality. His principles are still regarded as the theoretical basis to support social work practice in Japan without the slightest criticism. In a careful reading of his statements, it is clear that his principles are premised on the assumptions which place the client's subjectivity in a peculiar situation. He, as a clergyman of theism, tried to assert that clients must be respected because they are produced resembling the God, as divine (Biesteck, 1957, p. 74). Principles of acceptance and self-determination could be pursued only by assuming the rational mind as a given. These meta-physical explanations of principles are vague and not functional in social work practices. People who do not believe either in God or in the rational mind will have nothing to do with these principles. Furthermore, he himself accepted that these principles suffered from various restrictions in trying to adapt to actual daily life. In his conclusions, the client's self-determination was always reflected by the absolute rational mind but could not find the space to survive in the daily empirical world. Although he defined the client as, "in casework the client does more than merely cooperate; he is helped to help himself," (Biesteck, p. 6) and pointed out the importance of subjectivity of clients, the client was regarded as a passive receiver of help, and the social worker was essentially positive in their helping function. Social work practice which followed his principles has been caught in an inevitable dilemma.

In practice, the case leader is the social worker whose self looks on at a higher position outside, not from the client's perspective.

As a result, obeying more intensely the principle to respect the clients' subjectivity, confusion and distress increase even more, thus leading to greater malfunction. With regard to subjectivity in his theory, some contradictory points are mentioned below. In the chapter on the non-judgmental attitude, there is a statement, "When based on adequate diagnosis and a strong relationship, comments and interpretations about deviant behavior are appropriate and often necessary techniques." (Biesteck, p. 95). In spite of the non-judgmental attitude in principle, the social worker adopting an objective standpoint sometimes must lead clients to a better way of life, irrespective of their preferences. In the chapter on clients' self-determination, there is the statement, "The idea of each client's being fully self-determined must be modified by the realities in each individual instance." (Biesteck, p. 110). This means that certain restrictions are needed according to the state of clients, and the social worker is responsible for the decision to apply them. Individualization means that the professional skill of social workers helps clients adapt to various situations by virtue of their knowledge and experience. Six points, such as (a) thoughtfulness in detail, (b) privacy in interviews, (c) care in keeping appointments, (d) preparation for interviews, (e) engaging the client, and (f) flexibility, are listed as a means of individualization (Biesteck, p. 30), wherein the subjectivity of the client as an individual is never considered seriously.

Biesteck was successful in establishing some noble goals or principles which helped establish concepts for social work, however he was merely at the starting point as to how to actualize them in the empirical world of practice where dynamic changes were always being produced.

Change of the Client as the Goal of Helping

As Biestek said, "Since the removal or softening of the causative factors in the client's problem is frequently the goal of treatment plan, a correct identification of the causal factors and a certain degree of objectivity are necessary." (Biesteck, p. 27). Finding the cause, and offering services according to the function of officials in charge of the case was thought to be social work at that time. First, to establish a trustful relationship was the foundation of the helping relation according to his principles, and he used the reports of the casework services which directed environmental change and personality problems frequently overlapping with that of the psychiatrist (Biesteck, p. 6). However, how could acceptance and listening with a passive attitude function as an effective skill for the personal problems of clients? Rather, both client and social worker lose response-ability with each other and his principles do not give any concrete systematical explanation to change the problems of clients.

Although traditional social work has had a certain role, providing appropriate services for objective needs based on cause-effect relations assessed by the social worker, it has inherent limitations. In these days of data and information overload, family members can have certain problems in their mutual relations, even though they may be satisfied in terms of their objective material needs. In this context, the social worker has to step forward utilizing a new paradigm which effects change through dialogue. Thus the essential resources of social work are derived from mutual communication processes in which the definition of the circumstances is of maximum importance, although it is not always the case, as Bateson once wrote, that "they are taught that the way to define something is by what it supposedly *is* in itself not by its relation to other things" (Bateson, 1979, p. 15). Thus the role of the social worker is not just assessing the name of symptoms to the client, but the recurring *I* of the client in relation with others is arguably more important for long-term healing in a society where many live on their own.

Discussion of New Helping Principles

The new principles of social work practices are summarized below, in contrast with that of Biestek's approach which have been reached by discovering the way to make full use of the subjective self.

Aspects of I to Generate Principles

In order to let new helping principles function, there must be some agreement on how to utilize the *I*. Six basic points are listed below:

The construction of an I accompanies a statement of responsibility

In accomplishing thought or action with relation to others by the stance of the *I*, responsibly for assigning meanings to others is also implied due to the positive establishment of the actors. Furthermore it is quite clear that as long as the *I* is responsible for constitution and action, the others cannot essentially interfere with it.

The construction of reality develops according to I's own way

Speculation and action in trying to de-contextualize oneself from problematic daily life are constructed according to the subject's own meaning system, not according to true or false judgments on formal logic by others.

Constructed world is assured only by the practice of I

Constructing realities by an established *I* with response-ability to realize constitution and action is an indispensable practice to assure a life-world.

The reason for helping the I

When the process of constructing reality with others using *I* malfunctions, and the process stops and/or is restricted, the help of professionals to activate the subjective aspects of *I* is needed.

The content of helping the I

The actual way of helping clients based on principles utilizing *I*, is to contribute to letting the client explore the solution on their own towards a new constitution and regulation for the situation, since the client has reached a deadlock of constitution and regulation constructed by *I* itself. In other words, the social workers cooperate with clients to activate themselves in making differences in terms of definition of the situation and the selection for behaviors.

Principles of Helping

The process to construct reality consists of speculation by an *I* and the selection of related behavior, and is an activity aimed not at formal logic, but at logical consistency permitting diverse criterions for judgment. In this case, how has the constitution and regulation of the private rules developed? If the teacher asks his student, "Please bring this one and that one to me," the student will never say, "I will bring 2 (because this *one plus* that *one* equals 2)." The student reacts instantly and with little consideration for the teacher, because he or she has been already conditioned for what the teacher means with various constitutions and regulation of behavior. Furthermore, the process of constitution and regulation by client for constructing reality must be respected to the maximum degree for its logical consistency. Based on the aspects of *I* as tools of social work practices discussed in previous section, the three new principles are *The process of constitution and regulation, Infinite possibility* and *Exploring* I's *way*, as proposed below.

The process of constitution and regulation

The constitution and regulation of the subjective *I* deriving variously through those four processes listed below are specific in their nature, so that all the activities of clients must be respected positively to be determined not by the social worker, but by the subject (client).

1. The information process

Clients have had their own definitions of various objects around them through the linguistic system, for example, birthday presents from others must have specific meanings in terms of the sender or the situation, etc., and a person is sometimes treated as a superficial character or just as a number only to be assigned a certain role by the clients. In this regard, the objective view is useless, because whatever the objects are there, they cannot have any meaning for the clients without being internalized by their conceptual system.

2. The concluding process

Since the conclusion which is drawn has been well supported by Regulative rules and Constitutive rules based on private contexts of the clients, including such things as self, self-others, episode and speech act in constructing their reality, it is consistent with his or her deontic logic and must be respected.

3. The constitution process

In the process of constitution, some characteristic events suitable for the clients' reasoning are usually chosen intentionally.

4. The contextualization process

The process of constitution and regulation not only function to produce the context, but also reinforce it by collecting evidence. As a result, the produced or constructed reality is confirmed through these successive processes of contextualization.

Infinite possibility

In using *I* to elucidate the objects out of the flux of phenomena which are vast, universal reality for the client is produced by the complex manipulation of constitution and regulation. The way to elucidate and to arrange objects depends on the *I* and is always infinite in terms of possibility. This provides inexhaustible materials to be interpreted as shown in daily life communication noted below.

When an apple falls from the dish of a child, in what way will communication of family expand afterward? Asking members of the family about what happened, they may explain the situation variously by punctuating the series of events at arbitrary points to reinforce their own contexts. The parent might define the situation as the interpretation that the child was careless, only taking certain elements based on the context of parent-child relationship, and say to the child, "Be careful." On the other hand, the child might also conclude that the parent was overly cautious, looking back on the similar event in the past. It is unimaginable that merely the Newtonian law of universal gravitation as formal logic is sufficient for the family members to explain the situation. Nevertheless, their constructions of the reality are not only various in style, but also logically consistent for each member.

Exploring I's way

In the events of daily life, not the objective but rather the subjective way of meaning construction based on the subject's own context is worth being explored in relational communication. Nevertheless, there is still a rigid belief by most social workers that formal logic is the only rational way to analyze phenomena. If clients learn fully how to make constitution based on formal logic, will they then be able to consider an adequate way to achieve better adaptation for their environment? In the following sentences, whether or not the rational way of formal logic is helpful in social work practices or not is discussed. Symbolic logic has logic connectives such as negation, conjunction, disjunction and condition to make rational inference, and holds that it is not the content of proposition under consideration but the rationality of form which is critical to make true or false determinations.

Modus ponens (affirming the antecedent) as a typical example of an inference rule which consists of those components below.

1. Proposition: If p, then q.
2. Proposition: p
3. Conclusion: therefore, q

Affirming the antecedent: ((If p, then q) p) q

It can be transferred to the daily life situation as follows:
1. Proposition: If I say something to my mother, then my mother gets angry.
2. Proposition: I say something to my mother.
3. Conclusion: Therefore, my mother gets angry.

This is affirming the antecedent: ((If I say something to my mother, then my mother gets angry). I say something to my mother.) Therefore, my mother gets angry.

These explanations are true in the sense of formal logic, but do not elucidate anything that happened in the dynamic process of daily life communication in which each person gives specific explanations for the word said, or for the reaction subjectively selected, such that it is indispensable to trace *I*'s way to explore the specific rules by which the reality was constructed.

With regard to this process, Bateson offered the concept of "two stochastic systems in understanding the co-incidences of genetic and somatic change, which work at different logical typing, fit together in to a single ongoing biosphere" (Bateson, 1979, p. 141). This conceptualization can be metaphorically applied to our daily communications in which we simply blend both the system of narrow logic and the assemblies of private incidents to make statements out of necessity.

In other words, helping principles assuming objective rationality and formal logic of clients ends up in a metaphysical world in which no one can ever find an effective way to deal with things. If we accept that both social worker and client belong to an empirical world and that *I* is a discourse tool by which the self is lifted in the metaphysical world, exploring *I*'s way to construct the reality of the client is theoretically justified without harming their dignity. In this regard, Gergen and Kaye remark "Thus, to shift in the form and content of self-narration from one relation to another is neither deceitful nor self-serving. Rather, it is to honor the various modes of relationship in which one is enmeshed" (1992, p.180). Skills to accomplish the principles in practice are suggested in the later section.

Skills to Change the Problems of Clients

If we accept the frame that the subject could only indeed exist when contrasted by the object, the social worker as object is needed for the client to become a subject in mutual dialogue, and vice versa. As shown in Figure 2.2., clients can be the subject to respond, only when their Constitutive rules and Regulative rules are engaged by the counterpart of the dialogue. Furthermore, it must be pointed that what the social worker is trying to accept from the clients is not only the content of description but also his or her rules of reflection. These form the foundation to promote re-description of clients to construct a new reality, restoring response-ability of the client. And it is the task of the social worker to know how to select and to transmit the message which has the potential to change the setting of problems, strengthening the response-ability of clients by situating practice on two wheels of the principles and the skills.

It is the usual case for the client to insist on fairness of the problem definition from a logical and objective standpoint, even if it is merely an assumption. The social worker, accepting I's logical explanation for the problems and respecting the ability for it, utilizes the skill of tracking for further reinforcement for logical consistency of I. Tracking is the skill to resolve the previous episode of the client into the basic elements of the reality and to arrange them selectively according to the time series to achieve the sequence with more logical reality through the interview, in which enforcement of more logical I by the client is pursued with the support of the social worker.

That the meaning of the message is variously articulated by the receiver is the reason why tracking of the transactional process in daily communication has to be reexamined in terms of the consecutive process of act selection and meaning construction. Furthermore, it must be noted that the reality constructed freely by the client in these tracking processes between social worker functions in a sense as the still stronger logical restriction with only the slightest notice of the client, thus enabling I to select another way to finally change the rule; this whole process can be summed up as paradoxical. In another words, to strengthen and to inspire the logical I with tracking skills by the social worker is the theoretical basis for a subjective way to change the client, and in such practices the client sometimes selects the minimal way to change him or herself, even if the effect is maximum as shown in case studies (Oshita and Kamo, 2008, pp. 67-99, Oshita, 2008, pp. 101-139, Oshita, 2008, Oshita, 2010). The problem setting of the client is often vague and unbounded at the beginning. Tracking makes sense to give the problem a workable frame of logical consistency so that I cannot find another space to survive, even if I is given maximum responsibility and freedom by the social worker. In this paradoxical situation, I will try to make a secondary change to look for a new goal within his or her logically consistent program.

In contrast to *alethic* logic of syllogistic reasoning as true or false, Pearce proposed that, "In interpersonal communication, we need a logical form in which the statements describe whether we should perform certain acts. Because it deals with moral obligation, this logic is called *deontic* logic" (1994, p.14). By pursuing the morality of deontic logic, I can find the way to survive variously based not on *facts,* but on practical wisdom, i.e., good judgment. The social worker sticks to what the client says to the maximum degree with stimulating response-ability, and situates the solution as change of client's on the extension of his or her logical consistency, respecting I. Practices which respect the clients' logical consistency and achieve a change of their rules have been reported by Cronen, Pearce and Tomm (1985). Tracking of the episode happened even when the past is a creative process, because daily speech acts are done unconsciously, and assigning meaning to a single speech act in a dialogue with the social worker makes it possible to offer the possibility of another world of reality between them.

Setting of Problems

First it must be confirmed that in the process of deciding what to name as "problems", it is not the assessment of social worker, but the exploration of the client which has an important role. This is because the problem is not a matter of real existence but is an appeal of incompleteness which needs some problem solving behavior from the client. The harder clients try to solve the problem, the more painful they feel, and thus mal-adaptation is exaggerated. Once Wittgenstein said that "for an answer which cannot be expressed the question too cannot be expressed" (1999, p.107). According to his suggestion, the setting of problem with *I* and social worker is the most creative part in social work practice, in which the answer is merely arbitrary and could be dealt with in any way they invent. Clients grasp for the answer (which is named "solution"), even if they are not aware that their question (which is named "problem") this produces the maze in which they are caught. Of course, this being the case, the previous setting of problem by the client is even more supported by the social worker to inspire the utilization of *I*, because even in such a problematic situation, the client has tried to reflect Constitutive rules and Regulative rules of their own in the behavior of *I*. Thus the exploration of the new setting of the problem is placed on the same plane as how to utilize *I*, and that is the way to invert an unsolvable problem into a solvable one, respecting *I*'s way consistently. It could be suggested that problems are transferred to setting of goals. As Corcoran wrote, "Since no one holds the objective truth, individuals' ways of solving problems are unique and valued, and individuals have the rights to determine their own goals" (2003, p. 61). These practices are quite different from those practices in which the problem is ideologically fixed and explained only by means of causality or formal logic.

Solving Problems

It is *I* that finds the way to solve the problem, because the problem is constructed by *I*. What the social worker can then do in the process of interviews with clients is to transfer the message to highlight a difference in meanings of certain behaviors which are received or expressed. When a client in trouble can constitute a new reality with the social worker, finding another meaning to the behavior, the problem is understood to be solved, as said by Miller; solutions are interactionally constructed realities (1997, p. 68). Even if only one meaning changes, it can trigger the clients to find the solution as de-contextualization. Actual skills to promote a subjective constitution of the new reality are a sequence of circular questioning as reported by social workers in North America in the 1980's (Tomm, 1985) and moreover Solution Focused Brief Therapy (SFBT) by which the potential ability of the client to solve the problem is explored (Corcoran, 2003).

Conclusion

Although the self of client is respected in principle in traditional social work theory and practice, it has certain restrictions in empirical practice, due to a definition of the self which is rational with objectified existence. In our theoretical discussion, we see that the world is of supposition and is produced only by *I* in communicational process, in which primitive elements are bundled into groups in terms of freedom and responsibility. In this regard, three principles for helping are proposed: *The process of constitution and regulation, Infinite possibilities* and *Exploring* I's *way*. The *I*, therefore, lives in a world of freedom and responsibility in which to engage in the constitution and regulation of behavior; this is basically infinite in possibility, and the social worker helps the client explore *I*'s way to change insolvable problems into solvable ones in the client's daily communicational processes. We believe resources in social work exist in the process of dialogue to respect *I*, and the social worker as a professional specializing in relationships, activates the performative *I*, which has the potential to transform the client's future according to changeable circumstances on a new level.

CHAPTER 3

NEW PERSPECTIVES ON PROBLEM SOLVING SKILLS AND RESEARCH METHODS

KIYOSHI KAMO AND YUMI OSHITA

Analysis of Social Work Skills

Skills of the Assessment and the Intervention

The existing system of social work skills is first deconstructed and analyzed before a new set of skills can arise. Usually a client insists that the explanation of his or her problems is true according to their logical and objective explanatory system. The new type of social worker accepts the client's logical explanation of the problem, and then evaluates the client's ability for logical construction of the problem. This also involves constructing the identity of the client. The skill that encourages the most logical, concrete description of the problem for the client is the tracking of the event. Tracking is the most important skill to resolve the life situation into its basic elements which constructed reality. This tracking also rearranges elements according to a time series. Following the tracking activity, the intervention point becomes clear and the transformation activity of the problem begins. Because the client who evaluates and accepts the logic and the objective world tries to arrive at an exact explanation of the problem, the tracking will be accepted without difficulty by the client.

Of course our daily transactions are not maintained by rigid logical, empirical rules. Imagine a transactional situation where strictly defined propositional messages are transmitted; the interpretation of this message is still variously generated depending on receiver's meaning construction rules. The receiver might strongly react to the sender's non-verbal information. It is not always easy for the sender to understand the receiver's unique meaning construction rules.

The logical-empirical problem solving habit of the client often amplifies the problem. The client tries to accurately understand the cause of the problem generation according to the scientific causal model. However, an ultimate cause which produced the problem doesn't exist. Our life situation is defined as the consecutive process of act selection and meaning construction. Therefore, problematic situations have not been generated by an ultimate singular cause. Consequently, the attempt to search for the ultimate cause of the problem fails, and the problem that requires a solution continues.

Let's assume the following situation. A social worker accepts the strict logical explanation of the world of the client and encourages an accurate description of the situation. This client is then requested to explain the tracking data of his life situation in detail by the reflexive circular question skill (Tomm, 1985, pp. 33-45). This logical and empirical client seriously differentiates the various elements, and produces multiple meanings from these elements. Some meanings the client discovered trigger the solution, because the new meanings undermine the old world construction method of the client and the problem-solving process begins.

This method of this problem solving strategy is a paradoxical and de-constructionist intervention method. First, the client's practice of the logical problem solving is positively evaluated. In addition, this client is encouraged to logically and objectively describe his complaints by the social worker. The social worker then helps client intensively examine the meanings of each element of the transaction. Through this examination, the client differentiates meanings and produces new meanings which operate as a force which solves the problem. As a result, this client voluntarily abandons his original causal explanation of his situation and a natural process of problem solving is allowed to proceed.

This problem solving method paradoxically appears after the client's intensive logical-empirical analysis of the elements of the episode. This paradoxical technique to transform the client's originally constructed world by the client's own voluntary re-description of his situation is the most basic and important skill for social work. This is a new paradoxical technique, which must be differentiated from the original paradoxical prescription skill. The philosophical base of this intervention is the theory of de-construction. Such a social work practice advocated here should be regarded as the practice of de-construction.

The Systemic Principle of Social Work Practice

The Structure and Process of the System

The systems in which we intervene are the system of life situations (eco-systems). The eco-system can be shown in the Figure 3.1. as follows (Hartman and Laird, 1983, Laird and Hartman, 1985). This is a system which has the structure of interrelated subsystems. The dynamic changing aspects of system are defined as the process (Constantine, 1986, pp. 52-53).

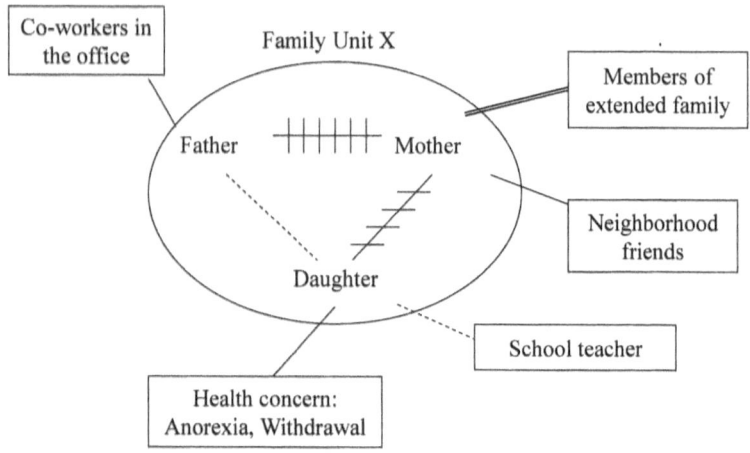

Figure 3.1. The Unit of Attention

The nature of the interconnectedness of family X and its outer systems is pictured using different lines (Laird, 1985, pp. 392-393)

If a social worker chooses the mother-daughter subsystem as the intervention unit, the social worker re-visions the complaints of these clients in terms of the system of the time series which consists of meaning constructions and behavior selections. This is interventions using the tracking method; the characteristics of the interconnection of this subsystem are assessed by analyzing the tracking data of the transaction between mother and daughter.

The Tracking Sequence

Figure 3.2. represents the sequence of tracking of the quarrel between mother and child.

Mother

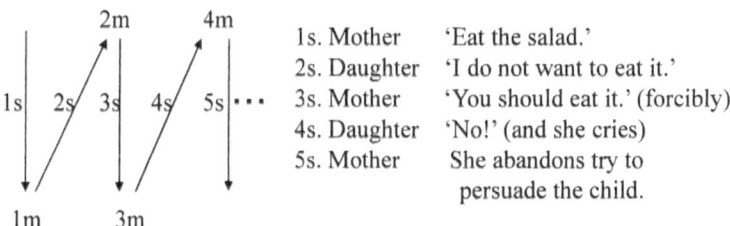

1s. Mother	'Eat the salad.'
2s. Daughter	'I do not want to eat it.'
3s. Mother	'You should eat it.' (forcibly)
4s. Daughter	'No!' (and she cries)
5s. Mother	She abandons try to persuade the child.

Daughter

Figure 3.2. Example of the Tracking

s: relational meaning of utterance, m: meaning construction

When the flow of the message from 1s to 5s is repeated, a deviance transactional sequence is therein patterned; namely, a negative feedback loop operates. The analysis is focused on a relational meaning of utterance and meaning construction of the sequence of this transaction. This sequence contains the meaning construction points shown by numerals '1m, 2m, 3m, 4m'. 's' indicates the meaning of interpersonal relationships of utterances which a sender may choose; 'm' shows the receiver's meaning construction of the sender's behavior. Specific unique rules signify contexts which direct both the sender's behavioral selection and the receiver's meaning construction.

Our intervention method does not adopt a causal theory which would presuppose the existence of a singular cause. It is the story telling by the client that creates the problem. If the client newly produces the act selection and the definition, the problem-solving process begins. This modified framework of Coordinated Management of Meaning (MCMM) which resolves an episode into a sequence of meaning constructions and behavior selection is our original intervention framework. In Figure 3.2., if clients differentiate either of '1s' or '1m' by his reflection, the transformation begins in this system. Differentiation is the general principle to change the system (Bateson, 1972, 1979).

Transformation Skills that Generate the Difference

Speech Act as the Object of the Intervention

The basic element of the assessment and the intervention is the speech act in the sequence of tracking data. For example:

'1s' Mother: 'Eat the salad' ⟶ '1m' Daughter gives a relational meaning to the mother's utterance (Mother is too oppressive, aggressive).

⟶ '2s' Daughter: 'I do not want to eat'.

We can identify three point of the intervention in this sequence. These are the point '1s', '1m' and '2s'. Assuming you are the social constructionist social worker, '1m' may be selected as the target for change.

We help clients reflect on their description and interpretation of the sequence of life events as follows. (SW: social worker, D: daughter, M: mother, RCQ: reflexive circular questions)

1SW: How did you feel about your mother's expression? (RCQ: *category differences*)

1D: Mother's expression was cruel and aggressive (=meaning construction of mother's utterance).

2SW: You felt your mother's expression cruel and aggressive. May I ask about your feeling of your mother's expression in detail? (RCQ: *category differences*)

2D: Sure.

3SW: What did you feel was most cruel in your mother's expression? (RCQ: *category differences*)

3D: The expression "eat" was oppressive (meaning construction to mother's utterance), and I feel anger at this. If mother doesn't force meals on me, I think I would not refuse all food. I would choose food in my own way if she said to me, for example, "You can eat your favorite things" (presentation of the problem solution act).

4SW: If your mother changes the expression, does your food rejection change? (RCQ: *temporal contexts*)

4D: Yes. I want my mother to not criticize me so loudly.

5SW: What will occur if your mother doesn't force meals on you, and she doesn't scold you loudly tomorrow morning? (RCQ: *temporal contexts and miracle question*)

5D: I suppose we will not get irritated.

6SW: (To mother) Your daughter proposed a solution including behaviors not to force and not to shout. What do you think about your daughter's proposal of the solution? (RCQ: *categorical contexts*)

1M: I am not confident whether or not it will go well. However, I'll put my daughter's proposal into practice.

7SW: So you are not confident.

2M: My daughter's behavior doesn't seem like it will easily change just from my behavior change.

8SW: Let's imagine that eating becomes happy for you and your daughter. What are you doing at that time? (RCQ: *temporal contexts*)

3M: I imagine we will eat while happily talking.

9SW: (To mother) Is such happy conversation difficult for you? If happy conversation becomes possible, what pre-conditions will be needed to achieve this happy conversation? (RCQ: *temporal contexts*)

4M: The necessary condition is that my daughter won't get angry at once when I say something to her. Of course I promise I won't compel her to eat, and I won't shout.

10SW: (To the daughter) What do you think about your mother's story now? (RCQ: *category differences*)

5D: If my mother does not attack me, I will not choose an aggressive behavior.

Intervention Skills

Basically these intervention skills are categorized into skills of the circular questions, and skills of a solution focused approach· These are skills that transform the world constitution of the client.

The circular questions

The strategy of the change of circular question approach is shown as follows: First, the activity to produce the transformation starts from the description of the situation by the client. The client is requested to describe the problematic episode (descriptive circular questions: DCQ). Tracking is the method to describe this process. Second, to elicit the change, a client is helped to reflect and differentiate the described data (reflexive circular questions: RCQ). The above mentioned circular question is used in these two stages. The categorical distinction between DCQ and RCQ depends on the social workers' intention when they use these questions (Tomm, 1985, p. 35).

Table 3.1. represents the outline of the circular question (Tomm, 1985, p. 40).

Table 3.1. Types of Circular Questions

A. Difference Questions
  1. Category Differences
  2. Temporal Differences
  3. Ordering a Series of Differences

B. Contextual Questions
  1. Categorical Contexts
  2. Temporal Contexts

A. Difference Questions

Difference Questions specify 'either/or' differences and temporal differences, for example questions on the differences that are stable/unstable, hostile/friendly. This question is summarized as follows. (1) *Category differences questions* ask clients and clarify differences of response to an event among family members, differences between interpersonal relationship, differences of family member's perceptions or ideas, and differences of relational meaning of utterance selection. (2) *Temporal differences questions* ask clients the differences between two time points. For example, client is asked for the difference of his mother's behavior before and after his hospitalization. (3) *Ordering a series of differences questions* is used to rank the behavior selections and perceptions of family members. For example, 'Who worried about you most? And who worries second most?'

B. Contextual Questions

These are questions asked about the relationship between categories of behaviors and categories of meaning. Furthermore, these questions inquire into the reflexive relationship between the levels of context. (1) *Categorical contexts questions* are the question that specifies the interconnectedness between levels of meaning category: the content of utterance, the speech act, an episode of interaction, relationship, life script. (2) *Temporal contexts questions* are the question that asks for the temporal connection between behaviors or life events. For example, 'If you did not hate your mother, how did you understand your mother's behavior?' (Tomm, 1985, p. 42)

Skills for solution focused brief therapy (SFBT)

The purpose of the circular questions is the production of differences in the old reality which the client has constructed. These are basic skills for social workers, and this approach is influenced by the idea of constructionist (Cronen, Pearce and Tomm, 1985). In addition to these circular questions, the social worker uses the techniques of the solution focused approach, when they try to accelerate the speed of the transformation.

Skills for SFBT are techniques that are intended to transform the pseudo-solution. The SFBT presupposes a solution based on the client's strength. Its attention orients the future orientation, and this approach values the small change which act as a trigger to transform the entire system. Solution-focused questions are skills such as getting by questions, questions about exceptions, scaling questions, and the miracle question (Corcoran, 2003, Nelson and Thomas, 2007).

A. *Getting by questions*

Getting by questions elicit the experiences of past or present successes of the client, and connect these successes to future solutions.

B. *Questions about exceptions*

Questions about exceptions differentiate the trouble situation of the client, and they focus the intervention on externalizing the meaning construction and behavior selection that has problem solving power. The more the discovery of the exception increases, the more the problem solving force of the client increases.

C. *Scaling questions*

Scaling questions ask the client to rank the externalized trouble episode and each of its elements on the measure (for example 0-10 measure), and this question enables the client to construct the solution story.

D. *Miracle question*

The Miracle question encourages the client to imagine a future miracle problem-solved situation (Miller, 1997, de Shazer, 2007). Using this description, the client concretizes the way to solve the problem. We use this question together with DCQ and RCQ.

The paradoxical intervention skills

When the problem maintenance force is strong in the system and the orthodox intervention does not have enough power to solve this problematic situation, the paradoxical intervention strategy is used (Weeks and L'Abate, 1982). Pseudo-solution is the repeated solution behaviors which function as the problem maintenance forces in the system (Watzlawick, Weakland and Fisch, 1974).

The example of the pseudo-solution process is shown as follows: Mother orders the daughter, "Eat the food". At this time, the mother worries about the daughter's physical problems. The daughter constructs her mother's message not as help, but the criticism and command. The daughter rejects her mother's help. The mother then becomes emotional and reacts to her daughter with more force.

To create a new solution, troubles are positively reframed by paradoxical intervention. For example, a withdrawing attitude is positively reframed as the ability to understand danger and avoid it. Crying is reframed as an action that honestly expresses the client's true feelings. The social worker prescribes and encourages the client to see that crying is a way to express feelings fully. The client takes the "I" position and becomes the subject of the world composition by these paradoxical prescriptions. Behaviors that produce the vicious circle disappear in the family if this method is successfully practiced.

Procedure for Change

The procedure for change is summarized as follows:

1. The social worker encourages the client to explain his or her story of suffering and to choose one problematic episode from this story as a target for reconstruction.

2. The social worker helps the client to describe a concrete sequence of his or her problematic episode in order to facilitate change in his or her rules of the negative story world construction (Malcolm, 1994). The client's explanation of one problematic episode is converted into tracking data which consists of the identification of specific behaviors and the meaning construction related to those behaviors. This is accomplished through the use of descriptive circular questions.

3. The social worker perturbs the client's or the other family member's act selection or meaning

construction through the reflexive circular questions. This intervention triggers the change of the dynamics of the transactional sequence (Figure 3.2.). Or the social worker intervenes in the client's suffering story through skills of the solution focused approach and paradoxical intervention skills.

4. The change of the dynamics of the sequence of the client's life event transforms the dynamics of problem production of the dyad (for example mother-child) or triad system (father-mother-daughter), through a systemic intervention.

5. Intervention in an extra-familial social situation can be tried in parallel with these processes. For instance, let's assume the intervention for a school teacher to improve their communication skills with students. This support is practiced by same procedure as the above-mentioned from 1. to 5. This is the intervention in the eco-system (Figure 3.1.).

Eco-systemic Social Work Practice

Because the place where the problem occurs is the ecological life situation, intervention that aims at changing the interconnection between family members and the outer system is needed. Then transformation of the family system and the transformation of the relationship between family system and external system are combined. This is the network intervention of solution focused social work in ecological life situation pictured in Figure 3.1.

Traditional social work defined the outer resources as the material resources. Our intervention instead defines the outer resource as the personalized physical resources produced within the transactional process. The *relations* between the family system and the extra familial system which provide the family with resources, decides the meaning of resources.

This chapter is aimed at clarifying the social work method to intervene at the eco-system level.

Measurement of Transformation

The Procedure for the Measurement

Gathering the tracking data

The starting point to solve the problem is to gather the tracking data of client's life situation using circular questions. The tracking data of pre-intervention is shown in the Figure 3.2. The specific interviewing process to gather the tracking data develops as follows.

"X" indicates wife, "Y" indicates husband, and "SW" indicates the social worker.

SW: [To wife and husband] How does your troubling situation usually happen? (DCQ: *temporal contexts*)

X: Our conflict situation usually occurs when I complained about our child. It happened yesterday, too.

SW: [To wife] Could you tell me about yesterday's situation in detail? (DCQ: *temporal contexts*)

X: Yes.

SW: [To wife] What happened first? (DCQ: *temporal contexts*)

X: I asked my husband, "Z always acted up while he was eating. I wonder how to deal with this problem (X1).

SW: [To wife] You said to your husband that your child always acted up while he was eating. After that, you asked your husband what you should do for your child, didn't you? (DCQ: *temporal contexts*)

X: Yes.

SW: [To husband] How did you feel about your wife's message at that time? (DCQ: *category differences*)

Y: I thought she wanted to get some information (Y2).

SW: [To husband] Ah, hum. What did you say to your wife after that? (DCQ: *temporal contexts*)

Y: I said to her, "For example, there is a way not to criticize him, isn't there?" (Y3)

SW: [To wife] What do you think about your husband's message? (DCQ: *categorical contexts*)

X: I thought he gave me some good information (X4) so that I said to him "Yeah . . . ." (X5)

SW: [To husband] How did you feel about your wife's message at that time? (DCQ: *categorical contexts*)

Y: I felt she expressed her agreement (Y6) so that I said to her, "That way, Z can eat without acting up" (Y7).

SW: [To wife] Then, how did you feel about your husband's message? (DCQ: *categorical contexts*)

X: I got angry over his message (X8).

We continued asking the circular questions to this couple until we recognized a typical pattern of deviance amplification as shown in Table 3.2.

Categorization of the pre-intervention tracking data

Each of the act selections and the meaning constructions that are basic elements of the tracking data are categorized according to the interaction analysis frame of Bales (see Appendix B; The Bales system of categories used in observations).

The sequence of the categorized tracking data is shown in Table 3.2.

Table 3.2. Categorized Tracking Data of the Pre-intervention

Subject	The elements of sequence	Categorization	
X1	Z always acted up while he was eating. I wonder how to deal with this problem	C7s	(1)
Y2	I thought X wanted to get some information	C7m	(2)
Y3	For example, there is a way not to criticize him, isn't there?	B6s	(3)
X4	Y gave me some good information	B6m	(4)
X5	Yeah....	A3s	(5)
Y6	X expressed her agreement	A3m	(6)
Y7	That way, Z can eat without acting up	B4s	(7)
X8	Y tried to force to me it	D12m	(8)
X9	I can't do as you say	D12s	(9)
Y10	I thought that X didn't understand the reason and was against me	D12m	(10)
Y11	You will get nothing if you don't do anything?	D12s	(11)
X12	Y criticized me	D12m	(12)
X13	That is all your fault, not mine	D12s	(13)
Y14	I thought X's response was too emotional	D12m	(14)
Y15	You should be more in control	D12s	

Note. m: meaning construction, s: relational meaning of utterance, X: wife, Y: husband, Z: child

Each element was translated from Oshita (2010). *Sapouto Nettowaku no Rinshouron (Clinical Theory of Support Network).* p. 102.

In the Table 3.2., 's' is the stands for relational meaning of utterance, and 'm' is the abbreviation for meaning construction. The data in the Table 3.2. presuppose the family system consists of mother (x), father (y), and child (z). Confrontations like this one often occur in the process of married couples raising children.

These categorized data are plotted on the three-dimensional graph (Figure 3.3.). At first, C7s (first) and C7m (after) cross on the (1) point in the above-mentioned Figure 3.3. Next, C7m (first) and B6s (after) cross on the (2) point in the above-mentioned Figure 3.3. This three-dimensional graph visualizes the conflict process increasing from point (8) to (14).

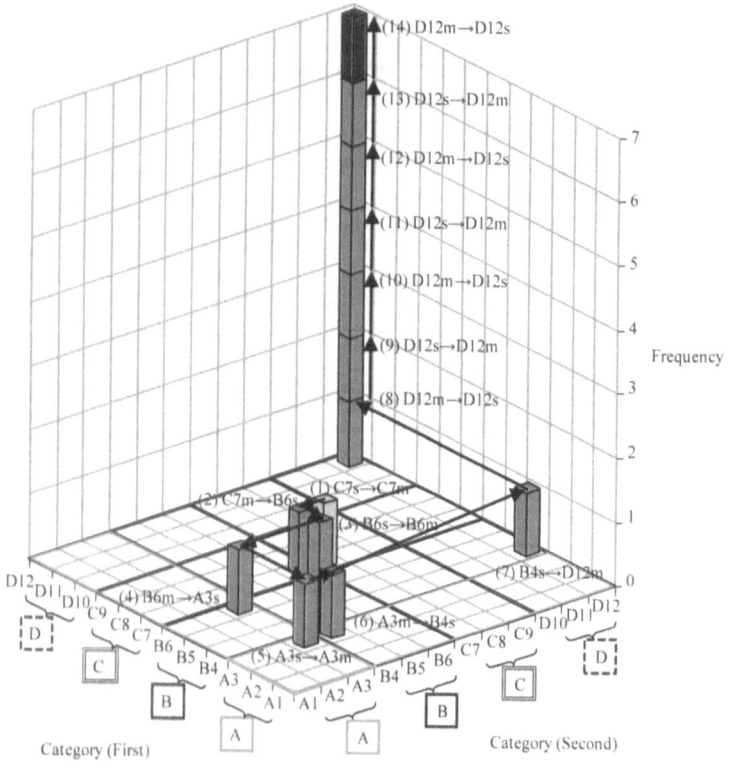

Figure 3.3. Three Dimension Graph of Categorized Tracking Data of the Pre-intervention

m: meaning construction, s: relational meaning of utterance
> A. Social—emotional area: positive reactions
> B. Task area: neutral attempted answers
> C. Task area: neutral questions
> D. Social—emotional area: negative reactions

This figure is modified from the one which was published in *Studies on Social Work, 43 (1),* 44 first.

Measurement of the deviance amplifying process in pre-intervention

Using our measurement model, we could formally define the problem of this couple as the increase of the frequency of D12s and D12m and the amplification of dysfunctional transaction between these elements.

Intervention

Based on our intervention strategy, the point where B4s following A3m generates D12m in Figure 3.3. is chosen as the target for change. Of course the intervention point is not fixed. Other points can be selected as an intervention point.

The intervention process using circular questions is shown in Table 3.3. "X" indicates wife, "Y" indicates husband, and "SW" indicates social worker.

Table 3.3. The Intervention Process Using Circular Questions

Y: I said, "That way, Z can eat without acting up." (Y7)

SW: "That way, (.........) Z can eat without acting up" (.........) [To wife] How do you feel about this husband's message? (RCQ: *categorical contexts*)

X: I felt that "Y tried to force me to do it" (X8).

SW: [To wife] You felt your husband forced you to do it. (RCQ: *categorical contexts*)
X: Yes, he oppressively told me to stop criticizing to our child. Then I got angry.
SW: [To wife] You were very angry, right? (RCQ: *categorical contexts*)
X: Yes. His way of talking is like barking. I understood it as forcing me. I can't accept such a forceful way of talking.
SW: [To wife] You can't accept his way of barking at you. (RCQ: *categorical contexts*)
X: Yes. I prefer that his way to send messages to me would not be so forceful.
SW: [To wife] Not so forceful (...). Can you give an example what method of transmission of his messages you would accept? (RCQ: *category differences*)
X: For example, if he says mildly, as my friend said to me, not to criticize was better for children. I would accept that kind of message.
SW: [To husband] How do you feel about her proposal? (RCQ: *categorical contexts*)
Y: Though I did not intend to order her to obey my advice, I know now that she understood my message as an order. I'll change my way of expression and transmission of my message. (.........). I'll accept her proposal. When I give advice about child rearing to her, I'll tell her more softly. For instance, I'll tell her as follows:

   "My friend advised me that not to criticize was a better way for children." (generation of new Y7)

SW: [To wife] How do you evaluate this message of your husband? [To wife] What would happen if he transmitted such a message as you wanted? (RCQ: *temporal contexts*)

X: I'll understand his message as effective advice, and I'll appreciate it. (generation of new X8)

SW: Mm-hmm. [To husband] I guess that this new way of transmitting the message about child care has the solution power of problems for raising a child in your family.
   [To both husband and wife] To verify the effect of new way of the message transmission, I want to propose the following practice. Do you agree to this proposal? (prescription)
Y and X: Sure.
SW: [To both husband and wife] You should talk about the problem of your child's meal habits some time next week. [To wife] You tell your husband that your child (Z) always acted up while he was eating. The problem is not solved though I scold him severely. I wonder how to deal with this problem. [To husband] Then you answer that there is a way not to criticize him to her. Moreover you tell your wife calmly my friend said to me that not to criticize was a better way for children. [To both husband and wife] Tell me how your transaction continues next week, after you have tried this new approach. Are there any questions?
Y and X: No. We have no question. We'll follow your prescription.

Through this intervention process, this couple could form new Y7 and X8 which has the reality construction force in the future as a result of the social worker's circular questions.

In the next session, they explained the result of the practice as follows. The wife positively evaluated the new message of her husband, and told her husband that it sounds great. This wife's message strengthened the husband's positive definition of their relationship. Then he said to her, "I'll do whatever I can do." His wife responded, "Thank you!"

Categorization of the post-intervention tracking data

Table 3.4. represents the elements of the sequence and its' categorization in the problem solving process, connecting the pre-intervention phase from X1 to Y6, and the post-intervention process following the generation of new Y7 and X8.

Table 3.4. Categorized Tracking Data of the Post-intervention

Subject	The elements of sequence	Categorization	
X1	Z always acted up while he was eating. I wonder how to deal with this problem	C7s	(1)
Y2	I thought X wanted to get some information	C7m	(2)
Y3	For example, there is a way not to criticize him, isn't there?	B6s	(3)
X4	Y gave me some good information	B6m	(4)
X5	Yeah....	A3s	(5)
Y6	X expressed her agreement	A3m	(6')
Y7	My friend said to me not to criticize was a better way for them	B6s	(7')
X8	Y gave me some useful information	B6m	(8')
X9	Sounds great!	A3s	(9')
Y10	X's message expressed her agreement	A3m	(10')
Y11	I will do whatever I can do	B5s	(11')
X12	Y's message expressed his co· operation	B5m	(12')
X13	Thank you!	A3s	

Note. m: meaning construction, s: relational meaning of utterance, Each element was translated from Oshita (2010). *Sapouto Nettowaku no Rinshouron* (*Clinical Theory of Support Network*). p. 115.

The categorized post intervention data are plotted on the three-dimensional graph (Figure 4.4.).

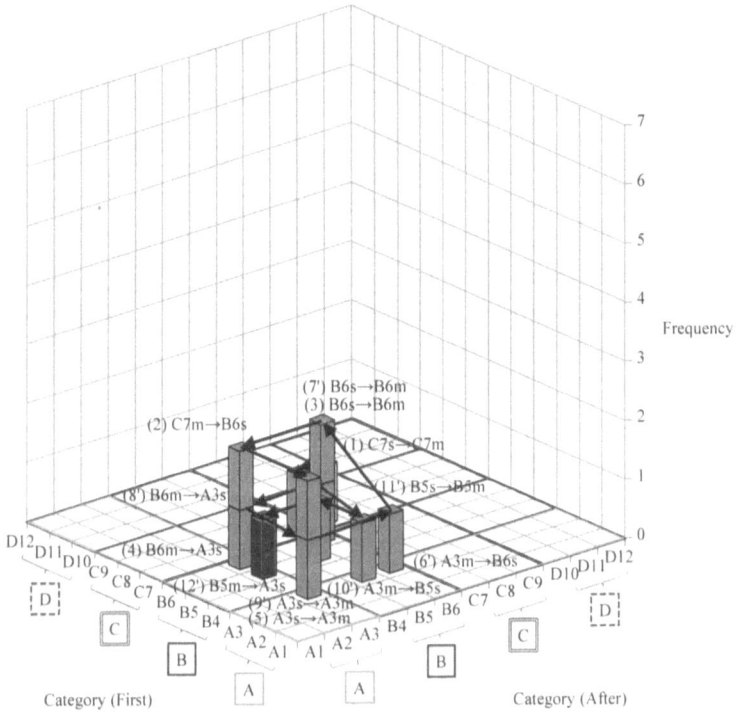

Figure 3.4. Three Dimensional Graph of Tracking Data of the Post-intervention

m: meaning construction, s: relational meaning of utterance
  A. Social—emotional area: positive reactions
  B. Task area: neutral attempted answers
  C. Task area: neutral questions
  D. Social—emotional area: negative reactions
  This figure is modified from the one which was published in Oshita (2010). *Sapouto Nettowaku no Rinshouron* (*Clinical Theory of Support Network*). p. 117.

Measurement of the new dynamism in the post-intervention phase

The differences of transactional pattern pre- and post-interventions are analyzed (Kamo, Oshita, 2008). We could formally define the problem solving of this couple as the decrease in the frequency of D12s and D12m and the transformation of the dynamics of deviance amplifying transaction between these elements. The measurement model of the intervention shown here is a unique model which exemplifies the social constructionist intervention method.

Conclusion

Based on the idea of the social constructionism, the data here provides an outline of the social work theory which specifies a method to analyze the mechanism of the occurrence of a *'problem'* in the life situation, and the skills to transform such mal-adaptation. In addition, in this chapter an example of the measurement of the intervention effect was presented. With the possible exception of behavioral social work, few approaches do what our social work model does: deepen consideration of the assessment method, provide an effective intervention technique, and provide a measurement model of the intervention effect. The effectiveness of this new social work model is further explained and clarified in the following chapters which present case studies.

PART 2

CHAPTER 4

SOCIAL WORK PRACTICE FOR THE ABUSED CHILD WITH HYPERVENTILATION SYNDROME AT A RESIDENTIAL CARE INSTITUTION FOR CHILDREN

YUMI OSHITA, KIYOSHI KAMO, KAYO MAEDA[1] AND HARUMI OKAMOTO[2]

Introduction

The aim of this article is to show the effectiveness of an ecological social work approach based on social constructionism. The situation wherein communicative messages are exchanged by actors in a transactional process is an ecological situation. From

---

[1] Kayo Maeda, MA., is a counselor at a residential care institution for children. This manuscript was written based on the research case of maladaptive behavior of children at a residential care institution for children in Japan. This research was conducted by Maeda, Kamo and Oshita.

[2] Harumi Okamoto, MA., is an associate professor at Bukkyo University in Kyoto. This theoretical framework was clarified by the discussion of our research team which consists of Maeda, Okamoto, Kamo and Oshita.

this perspective, a client's maladaptive life situation is defined by the story constructed by the client through pseudo-solution activities in his or her transactions. Therefore the hypothesis to bring about a change is defined as follows: if the client changes his or her story about the problem, the appearance of maladaptive life situation will decrease or disappear.

We have adopted a modified framework of Coordinated Management of Meaning (MCMM) which is a sophisticated theory of social work to help explain the structure and process of social transactions and enables us to analyze the dynamics of the construction of the problem by a client. Based on MCMM, the skills of the differentiation and the solution focused skills, are used to change the content of a story filled with suffering.

We have chosen to examine the case of a girl with hyperventilation[3], a junior high school student living in a residential care institution for children (Kamo, Oshita and Maeda, 2003, Kamo, Maeda and Oshita, 2006). This case was chosen specifically to highlight the effectiveness of our theoretical framework. The girl had suffered from chronic hyperventilation for a long time. The resolution of her hyperventilation syndrome complaint was effected using the above-mentioned ecological framework, and a specific de-constructionist process which discussed below.

Framework for the Theory and Skills of Ecological Social Work Practice

Theoretical Framework

Figure 4.1. represents the basic theoretical framework of our approach (MCMM). This is based on the concept of social construction rules. This framework explains the transactional sequence by two rules,

---

3   This case had already been reported in the Social Work Kenkyu (*Studies on Social Work, 31 (2)*). (2005) and K. Kamo (ed). *Higyakutaijido e no Shienron wo Manabuhito no Tameni* (Handbook of Social Work Practice with the Abused Children), Kyoto: Sekaishisosha (2006).

Constitutive rules (cR) and Regulative rules (rR). Constitutive rules (cR) organize the receiver's hierarchical structure of embedded contexts. The structure of the embedded levels of the context is explained as follows by Cronen and Pearce (1985, p. 72):

Life-script (L-S):	This is a person's conception of self in social action in life situations.
Relationship (R):	Relationship refers to a conception of how and on what terms two or more persons engage.
Episodes (Ep):	Episodes are conceptions of patterns of reciprocated acts.
Speech Acts (SpAct):	These are the relational meanings of verbal and nonverbal messages.

When we use the word speech act, this word contains both the sender's relational meaning construction (s) and the receiver's relational meaning construction (m) (see *Embedded Levels of the Context of the Social Structure* in Chapter 1).

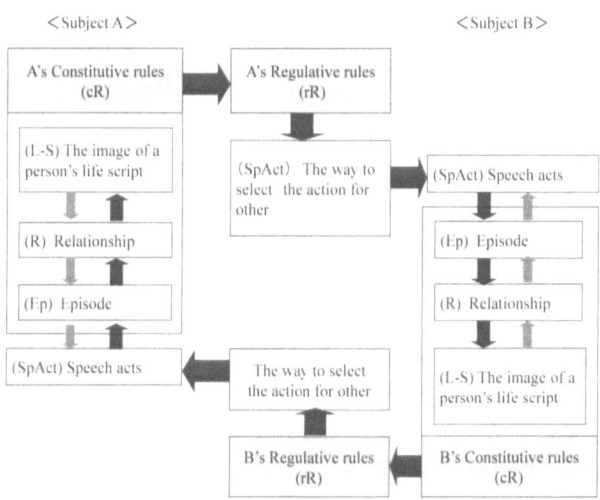

Figure 4.1. The Dynamics of cR and rR in the Process of Social Reality Construction

In hierarchically structured social systems, specific rules by which one level operates as the context to transform other levels can be identified. For example, the change of the meaning of others' utterances (SpAct) functions as the new contexts to change the meaning of the new Episodes (Ep), or the definition of the relationship (R). Constitutive rules operate as the pre-figurative force for the selection of the utterance (rR).

The other set of rules are Regulative rules (rR) that guide the utterance. For some persons, the rules of behavior selection are rigid and the actual behavior selection is pre-figurative and unchangeable. On the other hand, another person's behavior selections may be purposive, and the rules more flexible.

Strategy of the Transformation

At first clients are encouraged to express their grand stories of their problematic life situation, using descriptive circular questions (DCQ). Then one of the episodes from the suffering in the story as described by the client is chosen as the target of the transformation. Many effective skills are used to change the meaning construction rules (cR) of the episode in order to effect reconstruction of a new life world. For example, when the problematic episode is chosen as the target of the change, we can choose the "positive reframing skill" (Weeks and L'Abate, 1982) to change the negative meaning construction rules (cR) of this episode. Or another approach to reconstruct the negative meaning of the world is to have the social worker help the client to discover an exceptional positive episode. This is the so-called skill to explore the exceptions (Miller, 1997, pp. 78-79, De Jong and Berg, 2002, pp. 103-115). Moreover, negative meaning construction rules (cR) can be transformed by imaging the occurrence of the miracle in the future. This skill for recollecting the future success for the clients is the so-called miracle question (Miller, 1997, pp. 80-81, De Jong and Berg, 2002, pp. 76-102).

If the clients change the negative construction of meaning of the original episode as a result of the social worker's aid in positive reframing, this episode can be resolved into a sequence of elements of behavior selection and meaning construction of those behaviors. To realize a positive change in the episode more, the clients are encouraged to reflect on each of these elements. These are the reflexive circular questions (RCQ) (Tomm, 1985, pp. 33-45). Through these questions, the clients are helped to identify new solution behaviors. They will acquire new behavior rules to solve the problem (rR) through the repetition of practice of these new solution behaviors. At the same time, clients will produce new rules to define the others' utterances (cR). Therefore, the strategy of the change is summarized as follows:

First of all, the social worker identifies the negative episode in the client's life events, and transforms the definition of the episode through the positive reframing. Alternatively, he or she can transform the generalized negative definition of episodes of the client by using the skill to search for the exceptional episode. The client can use the skill to visualize the future miracle events to change the generalized problematic episode. In addition, the episode is resolved into basic elements through descriptive circular questions (DCQ). Each of the meaning of elements is differentiated by using reflexive circular questioning (RCQ). Through this differentiation, the new structure of the episode emerges (Figure 4.2.).

The social worker activates a trigger for the transformation of the world that is a system of episodes with the use of Solution Focused Brief Therapy (SFBT) skills and circular questionings.

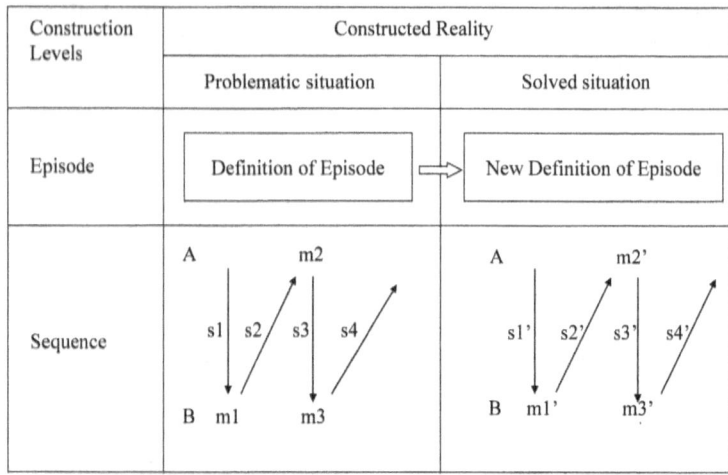

Figure 4.2. Creation of Difference between Ep and SpAct Level

s: relational meaning of utterance, m: meaning construction, Ep: episode

Case Presentation

Case Background

The client was a junior high girl (F) who had lived in a residential care institution for children[4]. She had a history of abuse. F's complaint was her chronic hyperventilation. Her symptoms appeared when she talked with her friend at her school about her personal problems.

Her symptoms were being treated at a pediatrics hospital. However, this symptom didn't disappear through only medical care, and F had continued to complain to her nursing staff about her anxiety regarding the hyperventilation. The symptom had rapidly become a serious problem both in her institution and in her school. A team composed of nursing staff, a counselor

---

[4] In order to protect the client's confidentiality, the names of the client in the case example described within this chapter and identifying background information are withheld.

(Maeda) and consultants (Kamo and Oshita) were organized in order to solve F's ecological situation (Figure 4.3.).

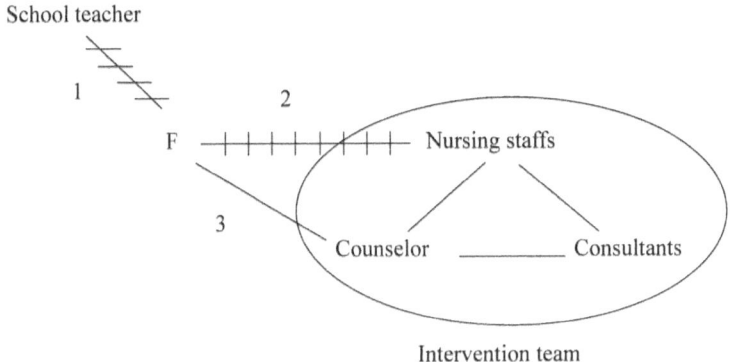

Figure 4.3. F's Eco-map and the Structure of Intervention Team

Number 1-3 indicates subsystem, ┼┼┼┼┼┼ Stressful, ──────── Stable

Assessment Data

F's complaints were made up within the conflict relationships with members of both subsystems 1 (school teacher and F) and subsystem 2 (nursing staff and F) in Figure 4.3. To resolve F's complaints, first, we needed to assess the dynamic of the deviance amplifying process in either subsystem 1 or subsystem 2. Then, we tried to gather the tangible elements of sequence between nursing staff and F in subsystem 2. F indicates a girl F and N indicates nursing staff.

1F: Why do I have hyperventilation? When I imagine the situation in which hyperventilation is caused, I become anxious.

2N: I think you worry too much about it. You should not worry about your hyperventilation.

3F: But . . . . , I feel my symptom is deteriorating.

4N: Don't pay attention to your hyperventilation. Do you have any worries other than your hyperventilation?

5F: In my classroom, when I thought about the serious illness of my mother, I felt strong anxiety. I don't know how to deal with all those things.

6N: Would you go to the child psychiatry department of the hospital if you feel that you cannot endure your anxiety?

In this data, the deviance amplifying process which developed between the nursing staff and the girl was assessed (Figure 4.4.). She did not know why her symptoms developed and did not know how to deal with the illness. She asked for help from the nursing staff (1F), but the nurses' method for solving her problem (2N) was vague. Consequently she became more anxious (3F), and the repetition of the nursing staff's solving methods (4N, 6N) was actually related to an increase in the severity of her symptoms (5F). The same mechanism was observed within the school system, as well.

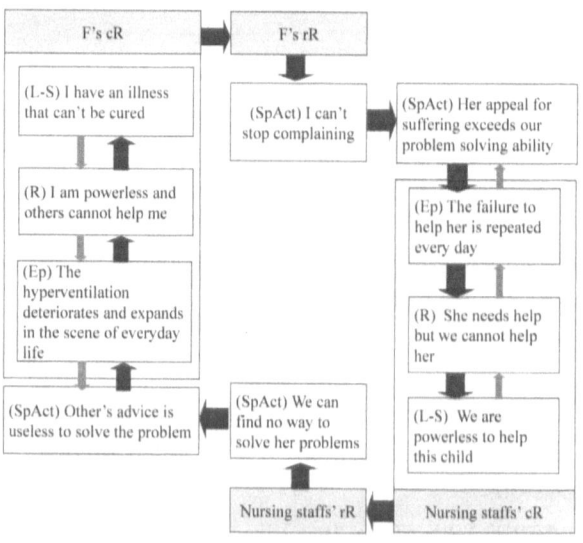

Figure 4.4. The Deviance Amplifying Feedback Loops between F and Nursing Staffs

Intervention Strategy

The team paid attention to the dynamics of the deviance amplifying transaction between this girl and staff in her institution represented in Figure 4.4., and the skills of circular questions and SFBT questions were used to interrupt these dynamics.

We planned an intervention strategy based on the following paradigm:

The purpose of the intervention
The purpose of the intervention is to find the problem solution activity of the client.

Selection of the Intervention skill
The solution focused problem solving skill is used to help the client find a new solution episode in subsystem 3 in Figure 4.3. In this particular case, the skills of exploring the exceptions, positive reframing and miracle question are used. Moreover, circular questions are used to help the client identify the element (meaning construction and behavior selection) for a successful episode.

Planning of the practice of the problem solution behavior
If the client can discover new solution behaviors by solution focused question, the client is helped to visualize and implement this new plan.

Reflection of the practice
The results of this practice are reflected upon by this client. Through reflection on the results of the practice, this client can acquire a tangible problem solution behavior.

Opening the Possibility for Change

At first the client was asked by a counselor to elucidate the temporal connection of her behaviors (temporal context questions) as in the following dialogue:

[Co indicates counselor, F indicates the client, DCQ indicates descriptive circular questions, RCQ indicates reflexive circular questions]

1Co: Tell me more about the day when you went to the hospital to be treated for hyperventilation (DCQ: *temporal differences*).

2F: I don't remember it well.

3Co: Well, do you remember arriving at the hospital? (DCQ: *temporal differences*)

4F: Yes. A little.

5Co: Then, what did you feel when you arrived there? (DCQ: *category differences*)

6F: I felt suffocation and feared what would happen next.

7Co: What did you do there? (DCQ: *categorical contexts*)

8F: I sat in the waiting room for a while. Then the doctor came to see me, and I talked with him. At that time, I did not feel suffocation (an exceptional successful episode 1).

The process from 1Co to 8F is an example of the beginning of the tracking process to solve the problem.

Extending the Context for Change

To help the client find a new resolution behavior, this counselor used the exception skill as described below.

9Co: What were you doing when your symptom disappeared? (RCQ: *temporal contexts*)

10F: My breathing gradually steadied while I was talking about my favorite movie with my doctor (an exceptional episode 1).

11Co: Were there any other situations in which your symptom might occur but you could stop it? (questions about exceptions)

12F: I covered my mouth with a handkerchief before entering my classroom (a exceptional episode and a solution behavior).

13Co: I was very surprised to learn that you have two skills you can utilize to stop your symptom (positive reframing).

14F: Really? (generation of positive L-S)

The client's complaint was resolved by virtue of a specific positive reframing communication process. The counselor's question 9Co had the power to extract the problem solving episodes from her life situation. She already had possessed the problem solving skill such as talking about her favorite movie when she spoke with her doctor (10F). Furthermore, the counselor facilitates her exploration of another successful episode (11Co). She could describe the successful episode and solution behavior (12F). However, she had excluded this solution skill from her consciousness. This counselor succeeded in having her unconsciousness surface to consciousness by using the skill of the positive reframing (13Co). As she found these problem solving skills by the exploring for exceptions, she began to change the context of her negative reality construction little by little. She started to believe that she could control her symptom by recalling these successful episodes and solution behavior (14F).

The solving method of talking about her favorite movie was one effective method to solve her problem. Therefore, the counselor began to explore more such exceptions in her daily life.

Elaborating the Sequence of Solution Behaviors

The counselor assumed that the old rule of negatively constructing the client's reality could be changed by her construction of the new successful episodes.

15Co: I believe that you will be able to control your symptom better from now on. Symptoms seem to disappear simply by recalling your favorite things, don't they? Well, let's recall something exciting in order to empower your control (miracle question).

16F: Yes!

These solution episodes were not enough to completely resolve her hyperventilation, however. After discussing it for a while, she found new problem solving episode. The following process was initiated:

17Co: What's your favorite food? (RCQ: *category differences*)

18F: *Zarusoba (cold buckwheat noodles)* (finding the resource of solution episode).

19Co: What kind of *Zarusoba* do you like best? (RCQ: *category differences*)

20F: Threefold *Zarusoba* in the restaurant (a happy episode in a restaurant that she remembered).

21Co: What kind of toppings were there? (RCQ: *category differences*)

22F: The first plate is sesame, the second is a plate of dried laver seaweed, the third is a plate of dried bonito (the emergence of multilayered problem solving resource).

23Co: It seems delicious, doesn't it? Let's assume that the symptom occurs again. If you sequentially recall three kinds of *Zarusoba* put in a threefold dish at that time, what happens to you? (miracle question)

24F: Umh . . . . it seems to be interesting (expectation of successful episode).

25Co: Let's call this plan, "Miracle *Zarusoba*." Will you try it? (planning to the practice)

26F: Yes, I'll try it!

Afterwards, the strategy to visualize the *"Zarusoba"* whenever she felt trouble was practiced on her own. The consultants confirmed that the practice of visualizing *Zarusoba* had the power to change the client's problematic symptom maintenance pattern, because the girl gave *Zarusoba* a new meaning, namely one which was defined as a tool to change the problematic story of the fear of hyperventilation.

The client could utilize three different visualizations, based on the *Zarusoba* Japanese tableware which has three separate levels in the dish. These three independent visualization strategies were useful for the client. If one visualization strategy was unsuccessful, she had recourse to use another dish to visualize.

This *"Miracle Zarusoba"* plan was shared with her school teacher to help practice when symptoms started to develop. F practiced the *Miracle Zarusoba* in both her school setting and in her institution.

Stabilizing the Dynamics of Solution

The counselor asked F about her progress after a while. She reported that she remembered three kinds of *Zarusoba* put in the three types of dishes when her symptom would begin to develop. She was able to practice this *Miracle Zarusoba* plan to effectively deal with her symptoms.

To stabilize the solving rules, the counselor asked her to describe her successful resolution of the episode into elements, and she was helped to extract the problem solving forces from each of the elements by the reflexive circular questions (RCQ). This communication process was shown following:

27Co: How were you able to do the plan named, *Miracle Zarusoba*? (RCQ: *temporal contexts*)

28F: It was successful. I could stop my symptom.

29Co: This is wonderful. Please tell me about your practice process in more detail (RCQ: *temporal contexts*).

30F: O.K! When my symptom seemed to develop, I recalled the three types of *Zarusoba* in the restaurant, put in three different dishes; they include sesame, dried laver seaweed, dried bonito *Zarusoba*. I imaged them in order. Then I could stop my symptom.

31Co: I'm convinced that you have an ability to control your symptoms (positive reframing).

Through the practice of imagining *Miracle Zarusoba*, her original rule of the self definition (L-S) and the meaning construction of episode (Ep) changed correlating with the emergence of new solution behaviors (SpAct). Transformation of the cR operated as the pre-figurative forces to stabilize the newly acquired behaviors of the client (rR). She gradually gained her ability to control of it (the emergence of the problem solving rule of rR, cR). Her changed reality construction is shown in Figure 4.5.

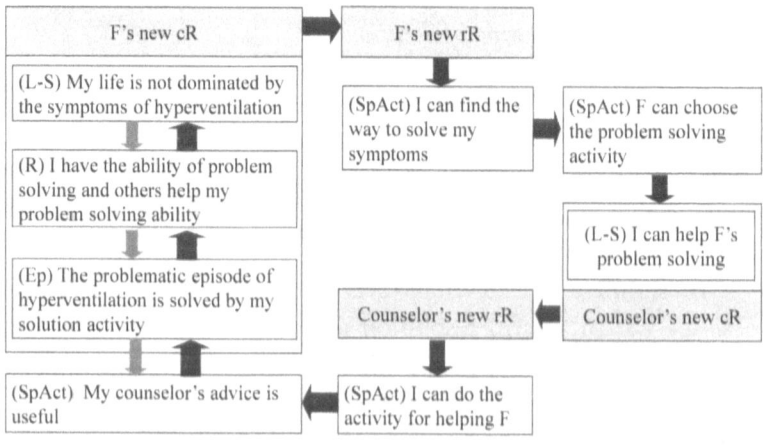

Figure 4.5. F's Problem Solving Feedback Loop

Summary of Subsequent Sessions

After practicing this plan several times, the girl reported to her counselor that her symptom disappeared. F's school teacher told the counselor that F's problem was solved. By this practice her new problem solving behavior rule (rR) was more stabilized. Correlating to this stabilization of rR and cR stabilized, as well.

Results

By using the skill of the exploring for successful episode (questions of exceptions, the miracle question, positive reframing, and circular questions for specifying the elements of successful episode), this client could visualize the problem solving situation. These problem solutions as behaviors had the force to construct a new self-image, new definitions of relationships; the new feedback loop between her acquired rule of problem-solving behavior (rR) and rule of the new world definition (cR) transformed the problem amplifying dynamics of transactions in her life situation. This simple *Miracle Zarusoba* strategy strengthened her management ability to her symptom. She acquired the problem solving rules through this practice and removed the fear of the appearance of this disease at school and at the institution.

Conclusion

The purpose of this study was to show the effectiveness of our ecological practice model that was constructed by applying MCMM through the case study of a hyperventilation client. Following the theoretical perspective of the assessment method based on this social constructionist viewpoint, we explained the intervention technique and its use. The main skills we chose were the miracle question, the question of exploring the exceptions, circular questions and positive reframing. We used circular questions together with these solution focused skills to describe the episode and to find the solution elements (client's utterance and the meaning construction of other's utterances) from successful episodes.

This successful intervention in the hyperventilation case illustrates the effectiveness of social work theory and practice based on the MCMM we are proposing here.

CHAPTER 5

SOCIAL WORK PRACTICE FOR THE CLIENT WITH HYPEROSMIA

YUMI OSHITA

Introduction

The aim of this article is to show the effectiveness of social constructionist social work practice with a client who complained about the hyperosmia[5]. The client had serious atopic dermatitis. Continual medical treatment was needed to reduce her atopic symptoms. Her symptoms were so severe that she had to be hospitalized many times each year to treat it. Consequently, she could not keep a full time job, and she has been living with financial support. Moreover, she complained of hypersensitivity of smell; from about one year prior, she had complained about the smells in her apartment. This hypersensitivity to smells caused her to have headaches, a feeling of suffocation, and dizziness. Consequently, she sought doctor's help because she couldn't

---

[5] This case had already been reported in the *Japanese Journal of Social Welfare, 43 (1)*, (2002) and K. Kamo (ed.). *Nichijo-sei to Sosharu Waku (Life Worlds and Social Work Practice)*. Kyoto: Sekaishisosha (2003).

endure the smell of her apartment any longer. Although an ordinary medical doctor might diagnose her problem as the "Sick House Syndrome", construction materials which could have been the cause of her hypersensitivity couldn't be identified in her apartment. However, as she lost her apartment where she lived, three weeks hospitalization and treatment for atopic dermatitis (as the official reason) was authorized for her.

At that point, her symptoms of hyperosmia were analyzed, not as a dysfunction of her olfactory organ, but as representing an existential anxiety similar to the sense of the nausea of the character Roquentin, in *Nausea,* written by Jean Paul Sartre (1965). That is, her complaints related to smells were considered as the representation of the ontological insecurity which deprived her of her identity. This also involved the loss of being in herself in human transaction (Laing, 1965, p. 47). The generative dynamics of this existential anxiety is easily understood by using a metaphor from economics. The owner of a commodity cannot know the value of the commodity until it is exchanged in the market. Similarly, in a communication system, each member of the system cannot know the meaning of their utterance until the message is accepted by the receiver. That is, the subjects of the communication cannot attach the meaning by themselves to their own utterances. He or she is thrown into an indeterminate situation; this is a situation where he or she feels ontological insecurity. To protect herself from such existential anxiety, she withdrew from (the verbal and nonverbal) world of human interaction, that is, she became a disembodied self (Laing, 1965, pp. 65-69).

If the social worker skillfully intervenes in the client's existential anxiety, this client will involve the skill of transforming the maladaptive defense of the disembodied self. This was the tentative principle of intervention strategy used here. Hence, a therapeutic interview aimed at transforming her rigid defense of existential anxiety by regaining her own subjectivity, and realizing her existence place in the world with others was tried.

Coordinated Management of Meaning (CMM) (Cronen and Pearce, 1985) was an effective theoretical framework to explain the meaning construction process. However, a comprehensive analysis of the behavior selection process was not contained in their CMM model. A mechanism of behavior selection process is therefore added to their meaning construction theory. This modified CMM (MCMM) was adopted in this case as a way to improve the client's adaptive strategy in a world filled with existential anxiety. The systematized intervention skills were also applied. Solution Focused Brief Therapy (SFBT) (Miller, 1997, pp. 79-80, De Jong and Berg, 2002, pp. 108-115) and the circular questions (Tomm, 1985) were integrated to practice the minimum solution, and the effectiveness of this practice system is shown in the case analysis.

Theoretical Framework of the Ecological Social Work Practice

Theoretical Framework

Framework of assessment

To explain the defensive maladaptive mechanism of this client, the CMM model is used. CMM theory is the social constructionist social theory which explains the social structure as the generative dynamics of the embedded levels of context from the viewpoint of rules in the transaction (Figure 5.1.).

Figure 5.1. outlines the assessment process in this chapter. The constructed structure of the client's complaints is assessed from two rules in the transaction; Constitutive rules and Regulative rules.

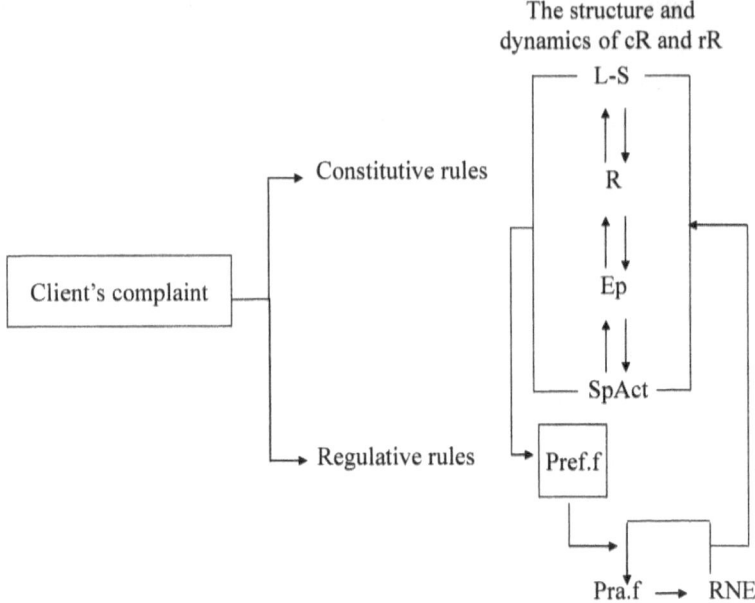

Figure 5.1. Basic Framework of Assessment

L-S: Life script, R: relationship, Ep: episode, SpAct: speech act, Pref.f: pre-figurative force, Pra.f: practical force, RNE: reflexive needs and effects

Constitutive rules and Regulative rules in Figure 5.1. are two main rules which guide the construction of one's reality according to CMM theory. Constitutive rules govern the dynamics of hierarchical structure of the contexts. L-S (Life script), R (Relationship), Ep (Episode) and SpAct (Speech act) are embedded levels in the context. For example, R (Relationship) functions as the context to create the meaning of the Ep (Episode). The change of the meaning of the Ep becomes the context to transform the old R in reverse. The following outlines elements of Constitutive rules (Cronen, and Pearce, 1985):

Life script (L-S):	A person's self-definition, for example, "I have no ability to overcome the problem."
Relationship (R):	The relational definition between self and others, for example, "I am suffering from the symptom, but no one helps me."
Episode (Ep):	The constructed meaning of events, for example, "My anxiety usually amplifies when I go to bed."
Speech Act (SpAct):	The subject's relational meaning of utterance, for example, He thought, "It was an act to attract my attention."

Regulative rules refer to a force which restrains one's selection of the range of action in interpersonal relationships. The structure of Regulative rules has three basic interconnected elements, as explained as follows (Cronen and Pearce, 1985):

Pre-figurative Force (Pre.f):	The basis of validity for selecting subject's actions to others. This is the precondition constructed from the generative dynamics of Life script, Relationship, Episode and Speech act on Constitutive rules. The subject's selection is restricted by the pre-figurative force.
Practical Force (Pra.f):	The power to respond, such as expansion of the choice of action.
Reflexive Needs and Effects (RNE):	Other's responses have the function of establishing the

subject's relational definition, and
have the effect of maintaining
or altering of subject's levels of
context.

When the term 'speech act' is used in the context of MCMM,
it contains not only the receiver's relational meaning construction
(m) but also the sender's relational meaning construction (s). For
example, I said to him, "It was hopeless." This utterance is labeled
(s). He in turn thought, "It was an act to attract my attention."
This becomes speech act (m).

Paradoxically, the more a client tries to solve his or her
existential anxiety, the more the client's suffering deepens. To
transform this vicious circle, the social worker assesses the cR
and rR which are basic rules creating the existential anxiety, as
the target for change. The change on one level of the embedded
structure of the context effects the generative dynamics of other
levels of the context (cR). This perturbation of the context system
triggers the transformation of the client's act selection rules (rR).
The process of the transformation of interconnected rules between
cR and rR is the process that leads to the solution of the client's
basic anxiety. Therefore, the strategy for improvement is defined
as rooted in a transformation of her world construction rules in
Figure 5.1.

Basic intervention strategy

To generate new rules of cR and rR in Figure 5.2., at first
the transformation of the old rules of cR is attempted. As the
intervention strategy based on MCMM, the client is helped to
differentiate the meaning construction in the structure of the
embedded levels of context in old cR. Then, the client is encouraged
to choose the new behavior (rR) in the new cR as a context. The
client imagines the resolution behavior being practiced in a real
life situation. The generation of the new construction of reality
and of the resolution behavior selection in daily life is reflected in

the session by the client. These transformation processes of cR and rR become the process whereby client improves his or her rules of reality construction and behavior selection which had previously perpetuated the existential anxiety.

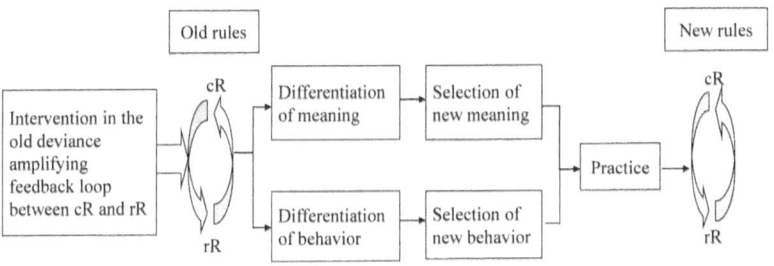

Figure 5.2. Basic Intervention Strategy

Strategy of Transformation

Figure 5.3. shows the dynamics of reality construction in a transactional process between subject A and subject B, containing the force of the exclusion of elements. The intervention strategy aims to transform the rules of reality construction by including those elements which had been previously excluded by the client.

For example, assume A and B as the doctor and patient. The doctor A says to the patient B, "Don't forget to take your medicine (1As)." This utterance 1As is not directly acceptable by the patient B. The meaning of this doctor's utterance is interpreted in B's old cR context which guides reality construction of B. If B has other contexts for interpretation, the meaning of the doctor's utterance may be defined as a different meaning construction. When patient B utilizes the meaning of scolding (2Bm-(1)) for the utterance of the doctor (1As) in B's old context of cR, B may consciously or unconsciously suppress other elements of the meaning construction as encouragement (2Bm-(2)) or great concern (2Bm-(n)). That is, the dynamics of meaning construction always accompanies the dynamics of exclusion.

B's meaning construction of the doctor A's utterance (1As) operates as a pre-figurative force behind B's response to the doctor A (3Bs). If B defines the utterance of the doctor A as scolding (2Bm-(1)), B will choose an oppositional act. If B negatively responds, "It is difficult for me to take the medicine (3Bs-(1))," it may become a challenge to the doctor A's original interpretative context of cR. The doctor may construct B's utterance as resistance (4Am-(1)), not as a request for help (4Am-(2)) according to the rules of doctor A's cR. The sending process of the utterance operates as the stabilization of the original cR, or as the production of the new rules for the behavior selections (rR). When the stabilized process continues, this process excludes contradictory acts (3Bs-(2), . . . , 3Bs-(n) and 4Am-(2), . . . , 4Am-(n)) from the original structure of cR and rR to stabilize its rules.

Then, this negative meaning construction of B's behavior (4Am-(1)) initiates a power struggle with the doctor A as the patient B tries to return to his original context with greater force. This strengthened cR directs the doctor A to choose his next utterance (5As-(1)) which is even more forceful than before. Doctor A may order B, "Anyway, take the medicine (5As-(1))." As a result, B's original meaning construction in response to doctor A is amplified, and this creates for patient B a further negative feedback response. Thereafter, homeostatic movement continues, Constitutive rules (cR) operate as the force for excluding the possibility of actualizing as a meaning of utterances. The focus of intervention in this example is the differentiation of B's meaning construction (m). This maladaptation process can be transformed by the intervention to help the doctor to reflect on his behavior selection (s).

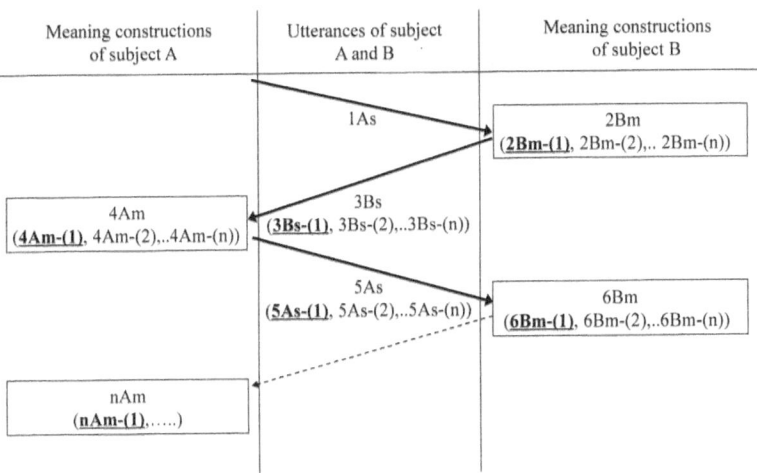

Figure 5.3. Transactional Process of Reality Construction

s: relational meaning of utterance, m: meaning construction, A, B: subject, 1-n: time line, (1), (2), . . . (n): relational meaning of utterances and meaning constructions that have the possibility of realization

The speech act is selectively created by the person in the context of cR and rR. We can define the world construction process as the feedback loop process between the institutionalization of rules and speech acts as the first axiom of the world construction. When the subject's reality is constructed as a difficult reality to solve from the position of ontological insecurity, a large number of the deviance amplified feedback loops (DAFL) (Constantine, 1986) are developed in the subject's ecological systems. The DAFL is extracted from the subject's rules of reality construction of cR and rR. If we accept the first axiom, a second axiom is deduced. World construction is the selective construction which accompanies the exclusion of speech acts which contradict the institutionalized context as shown in Figure 5.3. We can summarize this reality construction process as follows: the world is selectively constructed.

Therefore, the target of the social worker's intervention is the elements which the client had excluded in the process of meaning construction, which has been based on two rules; constitutive (cR) and regulative (rR). These differentiated meaning constructions of utterance operate as the force which changes the original Constitutive rules of the meaning structure as explained earlier. That is, the world, as the system of rules for the structuring of meanings and selections of behavior is transformed by the person's various speech acts which consists of meaning construction and utterance.

The changing process of the old rR begins when subject assimilate the different actions that are not to be included in old rR. When the client differentiates his or her old speech act and gets the new speech act using the intervention skills by the social worker, the transformation of the transaction begins. Second, the social worker helps the client to practice this newly acquired speech act (new rR). Third, the social worker provides a chance to reflect on the effectiveness of the speech act practiced by the client. Forth, using circular questions, the client is helped to connect his or her effective speech act to other embedded levels of the context, for example, Life script or Relationship, and to construct a new meaning structure of the world (new cR).

Intervention Techniques

The specific interviewing skills of bringing to the surface a differentiated element of one phase must be mastered by the social worker. Moreover, the interviewing techniques to synchronize the different elements which emerge in each phase, and also the ability to amplify the client's ability to reconstruct the rules of a new reality construction are also needed.

In order to transform the unresolvable reality the client constructed from the position of ontological insecurity, and to improve the coping skills of clients, the social worker must pay close attention to the client's complaint produced in specific contexts which are seen as depictions of how the client constructs reality.

Through the use of above mentioned theories which enable the social worker to assess the negative feedback loop of reality construction that the client is trapped in, the skill of having the client construct the problem out of the complaint is practiced. This skill is called tracking, and it can transform the client's troublesome complaint into the continuous elements of utterances and meaning constructions.

The main interview skills for transforming the discourse elements are the circular questions developed by the Milan School (Tomm, 1985) and the solution focused skills by using in SFBT developed in Milwaukee (De Jong and Berg, 2002).

Circular questions are seen as multi-dimensional questions for helping clients find differences in the meaning construction and utterance production in the communication process. Circular questions are categorized into descriptive circular question (DCQ) and reflexive circular question (RCQ). DCQ is the questioning skill used to describe the problematic episode. RCQ is used to differentiate the described data of a problematic episode by the client. Different types of circular questioning techniques exist for differentiating the patterns of problem formation and the temporal context. In this article, the social worker utilizes the circular questioning technique regarding temporal context to assist clients in differentiating the problematic vicious patterns and developing a new reality construction. The skills of SFBT are useful to reconstruct a new definition from the old definition of episodes. By integrating and using these two techniques, the power to differentiate the elements in a specific context, and the dynamic transformation of DAFL may be promoted more effectively.

Yumi Oshita, PhD, and Kiyoshi Kamo, MSW

Case Description

Case Background[6]

The client was a forty-five years old female called D, who complained that she could not live in her apartment due to her overreaction of the sense of smell. At the same time, she had been suffering from severe atopic dermatitis. Her olfactory sensitivity became so severe that the doctor permitted short term hospitalization as the official reason to treat atopic dermatitis. The real reason, however, for her hospitalization was for emergency support consequent to the loss of her apartment.

She came to see a social worker on her doctor's recommendation. Her complaint was that there was no way to solve her problems; she could not control her symptoms, did not have an apartment and the money to live after her discharge.

Ecological Assessment

Conflict amplifying in her life situation

The social worker encouraged her to explain her story of suffering in detail in order to assess the generative dynamics of her complaint. The social worker assessed her complaints of uncomfortable smells in her apartment as the symbolized expression of her conflict relationship with a public assistance case worker. A public assistance case worker told her that she could move into another apartment if she accepted the indicated diagnosis. She had tried several times to search for a new apartment where she could live. However, she could not get any information for apartments which did not have unpleasant smells. Only apartments which had intolerable smells emerged in her actual life, paradoxically in spite of her desperate attempts to search for an apartment that had no odors. Consequently, her

---

[6] In order to protect the client's confidentiality, the names of the client in the case example described within this chapter and identifying background information have been changed.

trials of searching for new apartments only deepened her world construction of existential anxiety. Therefore, she didn't accept the public assistance case worker's proposal for solving the problem at all, and couldn't discover any problem solving options. Finally, she was told that her rental contract was dissolved because of the fact that she no longer lived in the apartment. This also meant an end to her financial support.

Vicious feedback loop in her hospital

This episode involved her behavior selection of appealing to a doctor regarding her fear of odors. Her belief that she could defend herself only in the hospital as the fortress, became more stubborn by allowing her hospitalization. This defense was justified by creating an external world filled with uncomfortable smells, with the exception of the hospital. Therefore, the client hated going outside of the hospital ward during her hospitalization.

In such a situation, her ontological insecurity and her choice of maladaptive behavior which amplified the existential anxiety continued.

Assessment of Her Reality Construction Rules

Interestingly, she did not complain about the smell of the hospital ward at all. The social worker thought that the complaint of the odor in the apartment was a symbolization of the difficulty of her interpersonal relationships outside the hospital where her existential anxiety amplified itself.

The foundation of human communication is the exchange of verbal and non-verbal messages between persons. A sender's non-verbal message that enforces a receiver's acceptance of the sender's intention in the human communication process is performed through the communication channels which control non-verbal cues. For example, the accusing tone of the sender's message has the power to represent the mutual relationship between the receiver and sender and to elicit obedience from the receiver.

Specifically, in this case, the non-verbal complaint of the patient with atopic dermatitis has force which can put her in the dominant position in the decision-making process. Only by showing the client her serious physical symptoms, she could then control her world creation activities in her ecological system.

Therefore, the interpersonal transaction process of this client who had severe atopic syndrome manifested itself as the process where foul odors continually occurred. The client defined the meaning about the information introjected from the transaction process as the foul smells which she couldn't endure. This socially constructed foul odor extended not only to the interpersonal meaning construction of messages, but even to the material world, as well. In this case, the construction material of the apartment became part of the context of the communication.

As described earlier, the interpersonal transaction processes can be explained from the viewpoint of the structuring of two rules. The change of the dynamics of structuring in one of the subsystems triggers the structuring of rules of other subsystems. Then the dynamics of this structurization developed in each subsystem in her ecological system.

The social worker encouraged the client to describe a particular sequence of messages between a public assistance case worker and D. The following process shows the set of data where descriptive circular questions (DCQ) were used. 'SW' indicates social worker (author), 'D' indicates a client.

Gathering the data

1SW: What have you done to try and solve the problem of the apartment? (DCQ: *temporal contexts*)

2D: I consulted my public assistance case worker about moving into another apartment because the room of apartment in which I live now was filled with an offensive smell.

3SW: What did the case worker say? (DCQ: *temporal contexts*)

4D: The case worker said to me, "I can't directly accept your proposal. So, I can't go through the necessary procedures for your moving, unless you fulfill the condition as I said."

5SW: What was the necessary condition the case worker suggested? (DCQ: *category differences*)

6D: The case worker said, "You have to find the room *'right near the hospital'*. If you can't find a room, you have to provide medical certification which proves for your social rehabilitation you need the room where a foul odor does not exists."

7SW: What did you think of the case worker's preconditions? (DCQ: *categorical contexts*)

8D: I thought that both the case worker's preconditions to search the apartment were too difficult for me to accept (meaning construction). Then, I desperately complained to the case worker (behavior selection), "I cannot accept either of them. I searched for apartments, but there were no apartments without the bad odors. As a result, I requested the doctor to write the medical certification, but he didn't write a medical certification."

9SW: After your reaction, what did the case worker say? (DCQ: *temporal contexts*)

10D: The case worker said to me that my financial support will be stopped if I don't obey either of the preconditions. I couldn't find a way to change the case worker's decision. The only option I have is to obey the case worker's decision faithfully. That's all.

Assessing the data

Figure 5.4. shows the D's reality construction rules assessed from the set of data where descriptive circular questions (DCQ) were used.

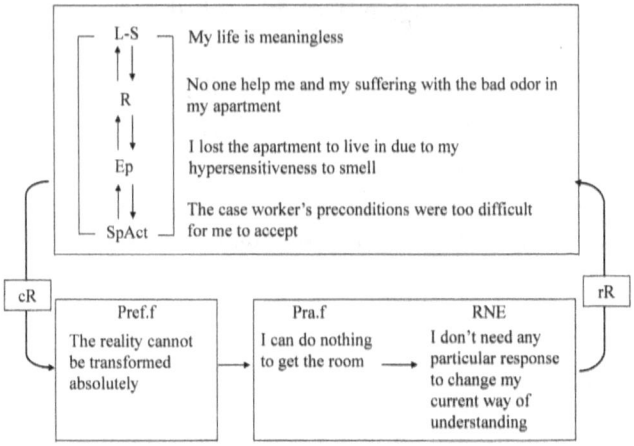

Figure 5.4. Deviance Amplifying Feedback Loop of Constitutive Rules (cR) and Regulative Rules (rR)

L-S: life script, R: relationship, Ep: episode, SpAct: speech act, Pref.f: pre-figurative force, Pra.f: practical force, RNE: reflexive needs and effects

Although the public assistance case worker offered two conditions to fulfill her request, the client D constructed the message of the public assistance case worker not as a proposal, but a restriction on the range of options and freedom of choice (6D and 8D). This negative meaning of SpAct in Figure 5.4. became a force to strengthen the negative meaning of episode (Ep), relationship (R) and the negative life script (L-S). Her cR of negative construction of meaning structure stabilized. This embedded structure of context operates as a pre-figurative force which reinforces the impossibility of any choice of behavior. She restricts the possibility of her behavior selection (rR).

As described to 10D, the rules of her act selection (rR) didn't have the ability to make another resolution behavior. 'Practical force (Pra.f)' is not differentiated by the client, and then the new 'reflexive needs and effects (RNE)', which operates as a new reality creation, did not occur. As a result, the old dynamics of the structure of the embedded meaning which justifies her powerlessness is maintained. This meaning structure (cR) functions as the pre-figurative force that restricts the selection of the new solution behavior (rR). Therefore, to solve her problems, the transaction between her cR and rR must be changed.

Her disembodied self was the result of her defense to escape from an existential anxiety. This defense mechanism can be analyzed based on the model in Figure 5.4. In order to maintain the familiar old reality construction rules, she rejected internalizing elements which trigger the change of these rules.

Intervention Strategy

To change her reality construction as shown in Figure 5.4., and create a new one, the following intervention phases were planned. The purpose of the first phase is to perturb the basic principle of her old reality construction (cR). The old meaning construction as a restriction which the client gives to the public assistance case worker's message '*right near the hospital*' is selected as the target for change. The second phase is to connect this transformation of the meaning construction to the client's new behavior selection. The third phase is to help the client organize the new reality construction rules between cR and rR. Through these intervention phases, the radical change of her defense to escape from her existential anxiety will be produced.

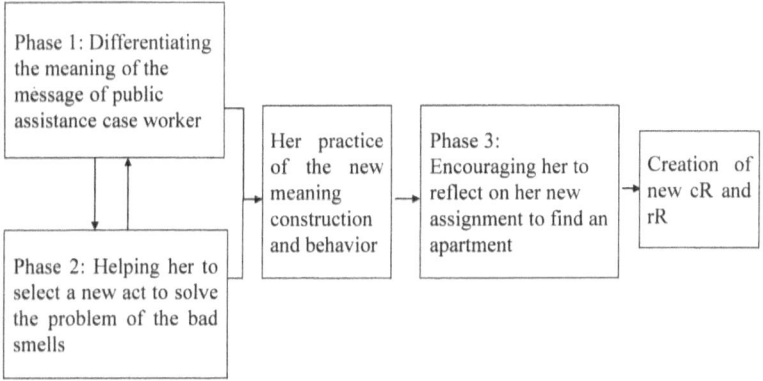

Figure 5.5. Intervention Strategy for Transformation of D's Reality Construction

The Intervention Process

Phase 1: The possibility of the change

SW asked her the definition of *'right near the hospital'* in order to reconstruct the client's meaning of the public assistance case worker's advice to find an apartment nearby using reflexive circular questions (RCQ).

11SW: Could you explain your definition of *'right near the hospital'*? (RCQ: *category contexts*)

12D: I was thinking of town A, B, and C.

13SW: What will happen if you investigated from one side to the other side thoroughly in those three towns? (RCQ: *temporal contexts*)

14D: I've already done that several months earlier. There was no house I could live in, in those three areas.

15SW: Certainly you have done this, I think . . . . , well, what will it happen to you if you seek in the neighbor towns near A, B or C towns? (RCQ: *temporal contexts*)

16D: Um? . . . . , well, . . . I don't think that I can find a new apartment in those towns, either. Moreover, those towns are no longer defined as an area right near the hospital.

17SW: Even if you can't find any apartment in towns near A, B and C towns, you can continue to your search to other neighboring towns until you find apartment that you can live in. That way, the apartment that you found becomes an apartment *'right near the hospital'*. Don't you think so? (RCQ: *categorical contexts*)

18D: That's right!

In this process, she abandoned her old restrictive definition of *'right near the hospital'* and developed the practical ability to redefine the meaning of 'right near the hospital'. She developed the ability to differentiate the meaning of the public assistance case worker's message.

Phase 2: Practice to search the apartment

In phase 1, she found the ability to differentiate or reinterpret the public assistance case worker's message to search for a new apartment. That is, the D's cR started to differentiate. The next step was to search her new behavior selection by using the pre-figurative force of this new cR.

19SW: Do you have some idea how to search for your apartment from now? (RCQ: *category differences*)

20D: I will leave the judgment of the conditions to the staff of real estate agents as it has always been in the past.

21SW: What judgment of conditions will you leave to the staffs of the real estate agents? (RCQ: *category differences*)

22D: I will leave the judgment about the rent, European style and the existence of uncomfortable smells.

23SW: What will occur? (RCQ: *temporal contexts*)

24D: Most real estate agents may say to me that they don't have any apartment where there are no smells, some real estate agency staff will introduce me to a room where they think an odor does not exist. However, when I go to smell the apartment, in fact, each apartment certainly has an intolerable smell for me. There has been a perception gap about smells between other people and me since before, I think.

25SW: You have great realization! I think that you have a special ability to classify smells in detail (positive reframing). What do you think about using a way of classification of the smell by making the most of your special ability? Which of the two ways do you think is better when searching for an apartment—either classifying smells according to your own judgment criteria, or judging according to the real estate agency staff's dichotomous criteria of odor? (RCQ: *category differences*)

26D: I think the classification of smells is better than dichotomous thinking. I'll be able to classify the level of smells, so, classifying the level of smell is a better way than the dichotomous thinking, I think. I'll try to smell all apartments which the real estate agents listed using this new way.

In phase 2, she could choose the solution behavior that clarifies the evaluation of the odor in the apartment by utilizing the future oriented circular questions, category differences questions in circular questions and positive reframing in SFBT. The change of cR (Pre.f.) became a trigger to select the new behavior of smelling the apartments (Pra.f.). If this solving behavior is conducted in practice, her new rR will generate and the new rR will become an ability to newly create the definition of her positive self image, relationships, and act selection (new cR). This plan of classifying the smell of apartments was executed during the weekend.

Phase 3: Activation of the new feedback loop between cR and rR

At the beginning of the next week, a reflexive interview on her practice was held in order to assess and reinforce the new feedback loop between cR and rR.

27SW: Could you explain the results of your practice? (DCQ: *temporal contexts*)

28D: I smelled all the apartments in A, B and C town that the staff of the real estate agents listed. All apartments had a fetid odor so that I had a bad headache.

29SW: Your effort to search for an apartment was wonderful. You had continued to smell the apartments until you got a bad headache, right? Then, what was the result? (RCQ: *temporal contexts*)

30D: All apartments had fetid smells.

31SW: Were there some apartments that you felt had a better smell among the apartments that you smelled? (RCQ: *categorical contexts and scaling questions*)

32D: I found only three apartments where the fetid odor did not exist.

33SW: Really? How wonderful! You could find as many as three apartments during this weekend? It was so great that I can't believe it!

34D: Still, I didn't decide to live there because I didn't have confidence to live there.

35SW: It is important to estimate the safety of the smell in the three apartments, I think so, too. Which apartment room did you feel the most comfortable smell? (RCQ: *category differences and scaling questions*)

36D: It is very difficult to answer the level and the content of the smell, but I would venture to say, one of them is the sweetest perfume apartment for me, I think.

In phase 3, using the scaling question, the social worker helped the client reflect on her solution activity. Through this self-reflective process, the client could find a differentiation of difficulty, which became a new method to solve her problems. As a result, she acquired the skill to solve the problem and her virtuous circle of cR and rR started to amplify.

Results

Through the social worker's helping activates using circular questions, the client re-defined the public assistance case worker's message as described in '17SW' (generation of the new cR). In this new context, the client became motivated to find a new apartment. Moreover, through the positive reframing skill which evaluated her ability to classify the smells (25SW), she began the practice to find a new apartment (generation of the new rR). Moreover, the social worker's scaling questions of '31SW' and '35SW' helped the client to clarify the tolerable level of smell (generation of the new cR). Through the reflection of the practice of smelling the odor of the apartment as shown in phase 3, a new inter-relational pattern of meaning construction and behavior selection occurred.

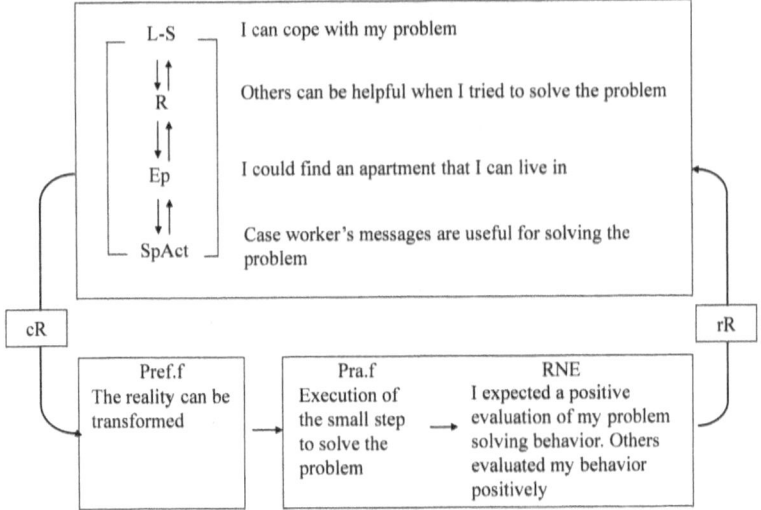

Figure 5.6. The Dynamic Process for Changing Reality

S: life script, R: relationship, Ep: episode, SpAct: speech act, Pref.f: pre-figurative force, Pra.f: practical force, RNE: reflexive needs and effects

The client's deviance amplifying feedback loop between cR and rR of reality construction was successfully altered through the intervention process (see Figure 5.6.). Thereafter, she could find a suitable apartment and leave the hospital.

Her disembodied self, which is the product of a defense to escape from existential anxiety, was changed through the transformation of the feedback loop between cR and rR, and the client's social adaptation level was improved.

Conclusion

A way to solve problems, both through the assessment framework, and the skill system of a new social work practice based on

MCMM, has been examined through an intensive analysis of an intervention with a client who had hyperosmia.

Since her olfactory hypersensitivity hadn't occurred in a transaction which was controlled by the professional medical staff, the social worker had assessed the client's complaints of olfactory hypersensitivity as a defense against a basic ontological or existential anxiety. Also, though not discussed in detail here, this client's fundamental insecurity manifested itself in an inability to have meaningful human relationships. To change her selective hypersensitive behaviors as a defense of her suffering life world, was the strategy invoked to solve her problems.

The main techniques which were used to change her defense were circular questions, positive reframing, and the scaling question, which emphasize a brief solution of the problem. The circular questions were used to extend the area where she could feel less existence of the odor. The skill of positive reframing was the intervention activity used to reconstruct the negative meaning of the client's behavior to positive meaning. Scaling was the skill to help her to find an endurable level of the odor. Thus these skills used in the problem solving process were effective skills in this case.

An example of the new paradigm of the social work practice which translates the client's complaints as the speech act in the human transaction was shown in this hyperosmia case.

Acknowledgement

I would like to express gratitude to the client of mine who was willing to agree to the presentation of her case included in this study.

CHAPTER 6

MEDICAL SOCIAL WORK PRACTICE FOR THE PATIENT WITH THE CHRONIC PAIN

YUMI OSHITA AND KIYOSHI KAMO

Introduction

A major theme in this article focuses on the representation of an effective theoretical framework, skills and the measurement of social work practice based on the concept of the language game (Wittgenstein, 1953) for a client who complained of chronic pain.

In this article, the complaint of pain is defined as a form of relational meaning of an utterance, according to the rules in the interpersonal transaction process, rather than as the description of a physical condition or psychological situation of the subject. Therefore, the key to solve the problem for a client with chronic pain is to alter the rules of the language game of the pain behavior which the client performs.

The Coordinated Management of Meaning (CMM) (Cronen and Pearce, 1985, pp. 69-84) theory that is referred to as a rule-based approach is modified. This modified CMM (MCMM) is utilized to analyze the dynamics of rule generation in the transaction process of this case. Both of the circular questions which differentiate the elements in the transaction process and the solution-focused skills which have the power to solve the problem, are briefly used to change the rules of the language game that maintain the pseudo-solution activity of the client.

However, systematized measurement methods for social work practice based on social constructionism have not yet been adequately theorized. Hence, the possibility of creating a new social constructionist measurement model to compare the transformation between pre- and post-intervention is discussed based on the modified framework of Bales' interactional analysis.

The client[7] in this chapter was a female who was diagnosed with somatoform pain disorder (ICD-10)[8] after surgical success on her large intestines. The sudden beginning of her complaint of pain was on the very day that she tried to temporarily leave the hospital for the first time after her surgical operation. The staff of her hospital ward performed a physical examination on her, but they couldn't find any evidence of physical pathology. After, a few months went by, however, the client's condition remained unchanged, and this case was referred to the social worker by the chief nurse.

The representation of her complaint of pain was assessed by the social worker from the viewpoint of pragmatic human communication (Watzlawick, Bavelas, and Jackson, 1967) as the representation of an unresolvable world construction that occurred in the transaction process in her ecological system. In order to solve the *'problem'* which had been constructed in her life situation,

---

[7]   This case had already been reported in the *Journal of Integrated Medicine, 13 (10)* in 2003 and in K. Kamo and T. Nakaya (eds.). *Hyumansarbisu Chousahou wo Manabuhito no Tameni (Handbook of Social Work Research).* Kyoto: Sekaishisosha (2008). In this article, consideration for creating a support network of solution rules which has not yet been discussed in that article will be explored more deeply.

[8]   International Statistical Classification of Diseases and Related Health Problems (ICD) -10.

the transformation of the rules of language game between the client and significant others was attempted. The analysis of the intervention process will be shown in detail, below.

Application of Theory and Technique

Framework of assessment

Generally speaking, the client's *'problem'* definition is constructed in the Deviance Amplifying Feedback Loop (DAFL) (Constantine, 1986). For example, a complaint of pain can be viewed as a speech act based on the rules of behavior selection of the client, and the speech act contains basic elements which generate the DAFL between members of a transaction. This is a radically different view than viewing the problem as an objective description of the client's physical and psychological condition. The particular utterance responses of others are elicited by the subject's complaint of pain as the utterance which has relational meaning in the transaction. In the repetition of that process, the rules of her unresolvable reality construction are produced.

The generation process of DAFL is summarized as follows:

1. Member A sends the message of his or her pain to member B.
2. Member B constructs the meaning of A's message.
3. Member B sends the message to A.
4. Member A defines the message of B.

To assess the generation of the language game provoking the DAFL, CMM theory which is a sophisticated rule theory is a useful framework. Using CMM theory, the rules of DAFL which are institutionalized in the transaction is analyzed. The rules are Constitutive rules (cR) and Regulative rules (rR). The features of two rules are as follows:

Constitutive rules (cR) (Cronen and Pearce, 1985, pp. 71-72)

Constitutive rules are rules structured in the embedded rules that govern the meaning constructions of the utterance of others in particular contexts. One level of this meaning structure operates as the context that creates the meaning of other levels. The dynamics of meaning construction of the pain complaint is analyzed by cR which consists of the hierarchically stratified meaning structure.

Regulative rules (rR) (Cronen and Pearce, 1985, pp. 73-74)

Regulative rules comprise rules that are closely related to a person's actions and refer to a force which restrains or expands one's range of action in interpersonal relationships.

Basic intervention strategy

The epistemology of social work theory and practice in our approach is based on the social constructionist theory, CMM theory and Bateson's concept of ecology mind. The social worker who can change the mal-adaptive social system and help the client to improve his or her social adaptive skills must have the knowledge of the particular intervention framework (MCMM) which is based on these epistemological principles.

The rules of the language game are constructed by the repeated transactions between members in an ecological system. The cR and rR are created by speech acts in the transaction. On the other hand, the speech act is guided by cR and rR. Thus a circular relationship exists between the speech act and rule creation. However, what types of rules which are generated in the transaction become dominant in the social system is indeterminate. Moreover, the dominant rules are not the objective reality.

The change of a rule leads to the transformation of the whole system, because it is like a family which maintains its stability by rules of cR and rR. The social worker activates a small change of rules by the use of intervention skills and perturbs the structure of cR and rR in the whole system.

When the social worker tries to transform the deviant social system, he or she needs the assessment skill analyzing the dynamics of the problem formation and the technique to change the institutionalized rules that guide the deviance amplifying behaviors.

Assessment, intervention and measurement skills

The basic skill of the assessment and measurement is descriptive circular questions (DCQ) that dissolves the problem situation into the elements of meaning construction and behavior selection according to a time series. These skills are deducted from MCMM.

The intervention skills are comprised of reflexive circular questions (RCQ) (Tomm, 1985, pp. 33-45) in the Calgary School, and Solution Questions in Solution Focused Brief Therapy (SFBT) (Miller, 1997, De Jong and Berg, 2002). Reflexive circular questions (RCQ) are used to differentiate each element of the meaning construction and behavior selection. SFBT interviewing skills are powerful techniques to change the dynamics of problem amplifying episodes.

Although these skills have the same theoretical roots as social constructionism, the discussion of how a practitioner connects these two kinds of skills has not been developed. In this article, the interconnected skill system composed of circular questions (both DCQ and RCQ) and SFBT is explained and the clinical usefulness of this skill system is shown through case analysis.

Measurement method

The data for measurement were gathered by using the tracking interviewing (DCQ) on the pre-intervention phase and post-intervention phase. By tracking, both of the intervention phases are resolved into the elements of utterance and the meaning construction. Each of these two basic elements was categorized based on Bales' category for the classification of acts of communication (Parsons and Bales, 1955, pp. 266-267). The results of categorization are visualized in the three-dimensional graph below (see the Bales' category in Appendix B).

Based on three-dimensional graph of the pre-intervention (Figure 6.5.), the generative dynamics of the problematic episode is assessed and the intervention point is chosen. After the intervention, the data are gathered from the new sequence of transaction using tracking interviewing (DCQ). This data is categorized based on Bales' categories and plotted on a three-dimensional graph as the post-intervention data (Figure 6.10.). The categorized elements of pre-intervention and post-intervention are compared. Then the transformation of the transactional pattern is analyzed between two of the three-dimensional graphs.

Case presentation

Case Background[9]

The client K was a female in her thirties who had been diagnosed as having somatoform pain disorder (ICD-10). She had complained of a chronic stomachache with nausea, as well as the impossibility of discharge and returning to her office. (Kamo and Oshita, 2003, and Oshita, 2008). Her complaint of this pain started when she tried to temporarily leave the hospital for the first time after the successful surgery of her large intestines. Before she arrived at home, her stomach pain became so severe that she could not stay in her house for even a few minutes. However, no symptoms could be found by inspection using X rays, CT, blood tests, and an endoscope. Despite receiving pentazocine by intramuscular injection, her complaints of pain continued, and she was unwilling to leave the hospital. Afterward, she was unable to make any additional progress towards discharge, and the hospital staff was unsuccessful in relieving her complaints of pain.

The social worker got a referral from the chief nurse after five months since the client had first started to complain about the

---

[9]   In order to protect the client's confidentiality, the names of the client in the case example described within this chapter and identifying background information have been changed.

pain. Weekly one hour intensive sessions were conducted for ten weeks with the social worker. On the other hand, the biofeedback therapy by the nurse was started two weeks after referral to the social worker. Moreover, an intravenous treatment (haloperidol, triazolam, perospirone hydrochloride hydrate and brotizolam) by a psychiatrist was begun a month after the social worker's intervention had started.

At the beginning of the session, the social worker encouraged her to explain her story suffering from chronic pain. Then the social worker assessed her ecological situation as follows:

Ecological Assessment

The client's ecological situation

The client's ecological situation based on client's story is shown in Figure 6.1. The client's complaints of the pain were generated from within the conflict relationships with members of both hospital subsystem and office subsystem. In the following section, the functions of each subsystem are analyzed in detail.

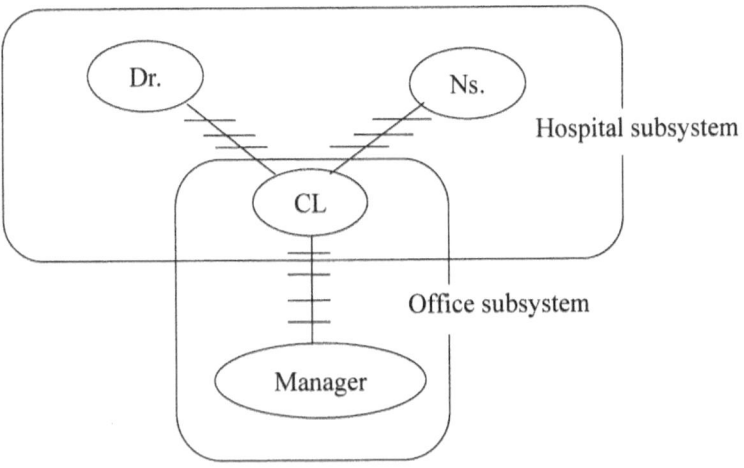

Figure 6.1. Client's Ecological System in the Assessment Phase

++++ Stressful relationship

Conflict amplifying mechanism in the hospital

In the hospital subsystem, the mechanism of deterioration of her solution abilities triggered by the two antinomic prescriptions is represented in Figure 6.2. The doctor diagnosed her pain as not being caused by only physical pathology but by a psychological one (1a). Based on his diagnosis, the doctor advised her to merely endure the pain (1b).

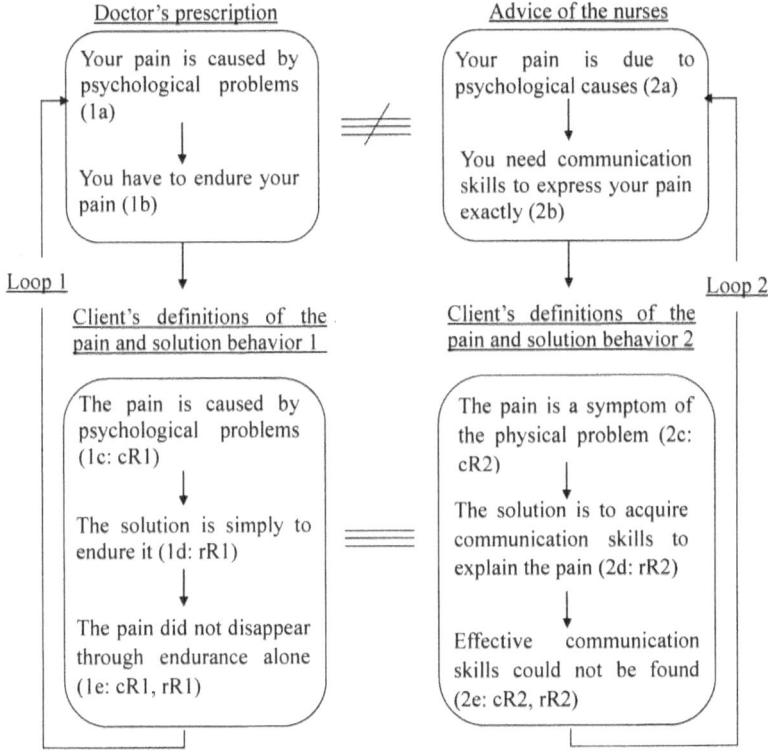

Figure 6.2. The Structure of Paradoxical Communication in the Therapeutic Situation in the Hospital Subsystem

$\not\equiv$: Antagonism, $\equiv$: Synergism, $\longrightarrow$: Direction of the force, cR: Constitutive rules, rR: Regulative rules

The client accepted the doctor's advice (1c) and attempted to endure the pain (1d). However, her endurance could not alleviate her pain (1e). The client asked the doctor for help for her pain. The doctor's prescription was the same as before (1b). Her hyperconsciousness to the pain increased even more. The vicious circle develops in the therapeutic transaction between the doctor and the client (loop 1 in Figure 6.2.). In this vicious circle, the pseudo-solution activities which aggravated the client's ability to cope with the pain continue, and her hyperconsciousness to the pain increased.

The other vicious circle developed between nursing staff and client (loop 2 in Figure 6.2.). The nurses, on the other hand, considered her complaint of the pain as representing her insufficient skills to express her pain (2a). Then, the nurses advised the client that she needed more effective communication skills for explaining her feelings about the pain (2b). The client agreed with this advice (2c) and tried to acquire some effective communication skills to tell her doctor about the pain (2d). Although she accepted this advice and tried to acquire these skills, she could not develop enough effective communication ability to reduce her pain (2e). The nurses continued to encourage her even more forcefully (2b).

Furthermore, a contradiction amplified in the team of therapy consisted of the doctor and nurses. This is the meta-level vicious circle created by the transaction between the two vicious circles (loop 1 and loop 2 in Figure 6.2.). The doctor diagnosed that the pain was psychologically caused. He prescribed that she endure the pain. On the other hand, the nursing staff explained her problem as being due to insufficient communication skills for expressing her pain to the doctor. The client had to accept both of the antinomic prescriptions and accept the solution behaviors of both staff prescriptions. Under this therapeutic situation in which contradictory messages were being sent, the client failed to understand the real meaning of the pain and couldn't find skills for problem solving. Consequently, her self-definition was constructed negatively, and it operated as a context to choose the action of appealing to the doctor and nursing staff to help her. Moreover, the contradiction intensified more between these prescriptions. They encouraged her to obey their prescriptions even more strongly. The contradictions intensified more between the doctor's prescription and nurses' advice. The client had to continue the language game of a pain that she could not escape until the end of her hospital stay.

Vicious feedback loop in the office subsystem

In her office subsystem, because a split and negative self-definition generated in the hospital subsystem functioned as a context for her reality construction, a vicious feedback loop operated between the manager and the client (loop 3 in Figure 6.3.). The manager judged that the client's complaint of the pain was her idleness caused by her long-term hospital stay (3a). Though the manager in her office ardently continued to persuade her to come back to the office during her long-term sick leave (3b), she didn't try to accept his proposal because of the seeming impossibility of following his advice (4c). Therefore, she chose to endure the pain as the solution behavior in order to improve her idleness (4d). However, she couldn't improve her idleness by enduring the pain. This episode in her office subsystem was introjected into her generalized negative self-definition constructed in the hospital subsystem, and the negative implications of her self-definition increased even more.

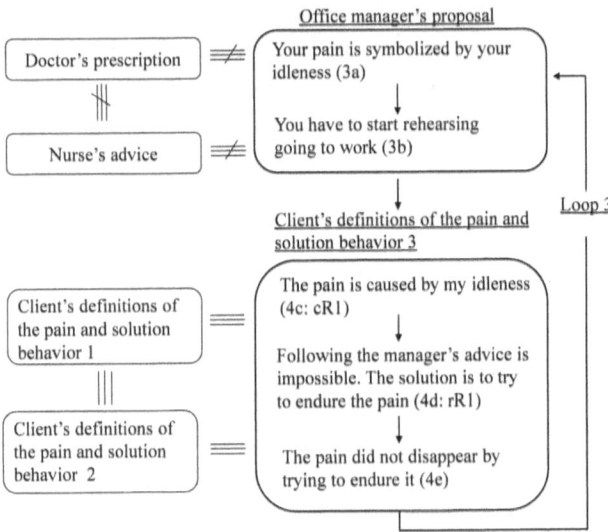

Figure 6.3. The Structure of Deviance Amplifying Feedback Loop between the Hospital Subsystem and the Office Subsystem

$\not\equiv$: Antagonism, $\equiv$: Synergism, $\longrightarrow$: Direction of the force, cR: Constitutive rules, rR: Regulative rules

In these situations, the DAFL developed in the transaction between the doctor-client subsystem, the nurses-client subsystem, and the manager-client subsystem. This DAFL split the client's existential mode and she lost the stable positive self-definition and ability to create the problem solving behavior.

To change this DAFL which consists of mutually interconnected three contradictory subsystems, two subsystems in the hospital were chosen as targets for change. The social worker assumed that the transformation of a subsystem in the hospital would expand to encompass a range of the whole living system. This was the basic strategy to help her to leave the hospital.

Intensive Assessment

The social worker required the client to accurately describe a particular repetitive situation between her and the doctor in order to assess the typical contradicted pattern in the hospital subsystem. The assessment data in Table 6.1. elicited from the interview by the social worker using the tracking skill (DCQ) shows the deviance increasing sequence of meaning constructions and behavior selections. In Table 6.1., 's' stands for 'relational meaning of utterance', and 'm' is the symbol for 'meaning construction'. The number from (1) to (8) in Table 6.1. indicates the point on the three-dimensional graph in Figure 6.5. that will later be shown in measurement of the phase.

As shown in Table 6.1., the dynamics of constructing the client's story were represented as the composition of nine elements. The rules of the client's language games are as follows: the meaning of the doctor's utterance was constructed as self blame. Then the client chose the action consistent with this self-definition. The meaning of the doctor's response to this client's utterance was constructed as self blame because she could not control her pain. After that, the doctor and client's downward spiral continued.

Table 6.1. Categorized Assessment Data of Pre-intervention

Subject	The elements of sequence	Categorization	
Dr.1	How is your condition, today?	C8s	(1)
K2	I thought the doctor blamed me	D12m	(2)
K3	I could not refuse to receive an injection yesterday, after all	D12s	(3)
Dr.4	You must not be reliant on painkillers. Your pain is not physical. You only have to make yourself patient when pain appears. Then you will be an outpatient. You should be more patient	D12s	(4)
K5	The doctor accused me of my impatience	D12m	(5)
K6	I can't be patient with my pain any more!	D12s	(6)
Dr.7	The only way to discharge you is for you to control your pain by yourself	D12s	(7)
K8	The doctor criticized me	D12m	(8)
K9	I can't do anything to obey you!	D12s	

Note. m: meaning construction, s: relational meaning of utterance, Dr.: doctor, K: client.
Table 6.1. was translated from Table 3-2 in Oshita, Y. (2008). Shakaikouseishugiteki Kouka Sokuteihou no Jissai. In K. Kamo and T. Nakaya (eds.). Hyumansarbisu Chosahou wo Manabuhito no Tameni. Kyoto: Sekaishisosha. p. 110.

Client's rules of reality construction

Based on the data in Table 6.1., the embedded structure of the client's cR is analyzed (Figure 6.4.). The mechanism of reciprocal generation develops between these embedded levels of meaning construction. $\frac{\text{L-S}}{\text{R}}$ indicates that L-S (life script) is the higher order context within which R (relationship) is understood (Cronen, Pearce and Tomm, 1985, p. 206).

According to Figure 6.4., the client's construction was explained as follows: in the context of Life script [powerless self] (L-S) as the highest order, the meaning of relationship 1 and 2 are born by L-S, the new meaning of Episode (Ep) is derived from the context of relationship 1 and 2. Conversely, the meaning of relationship 1 and 2 is established by the context of Ep, and in the context of R, L-S emerges.

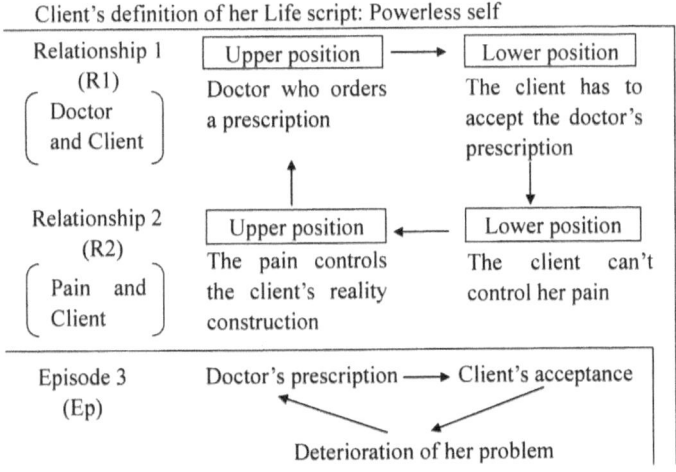

Figure 6.4. Dynamics of the Client's Construction of the Pain World

The [Upper position] indicates the subject's position or things which are personified by the client which take a controllable position in his or her circumstance. The [lower position] indicates the subject's position controlled by the other people or personified things.

As represented to Figure 6.4., in the relation between doctor and client, the doctor prescribed to the client the solution from the higher position (Relationship 1; upper position). Therefore, the client had to obey the prescription of the doctor (Relationship 1; lower position). However, this advice could not cure the pain. That is, the client was left behind in the situation wherein she could not relieve the pain (Relationship 2; lower position). Consequently, the pain occupied a higher position than the position of the client (Relationship 2; upper position). In the transaction wherein the doctor's ineffective advice was repeated, the pain occupies the highest position among the doctor, the client and pain; the doctor is in a higher position than the client, and the client is the lowest position among them. Her definition of the relationships (R) between the pain, the doctor, and herself operates as the context to create the negative meaning of her future episodes 3. The negatively constructed episodes will operate as the pre-figurative force to select her solution behavior.

Measurement of the phase

The categorization column in Table 6.1. shows the abbreviation sign that categorized each element in the sequence according to Bales' interaction analysis frame. Bales' interaction analysis frame has four categories. The alphabet A and D are the social-emotional area category, and B and C are the task area category (in detail explanation of these categories, Appendix B; The Bales system of categories used in observation). These categorized data in Table 6.1. are plotted on the three-dimensional graph (see Figure 6.5.).

The specific procedure for making a three-dimensional graph is as follows: the first piece of data in Table 6.1. is the doctor's utterance Dr.1, [C8s]. This message is to ask the client to evaluate her condition in his conventional fashion. The second piece of data is the client's meaning construction K2, [D12m]. The client interpreted Dr.1 as a criticism of her intolerance of pain in the context of negative life script (L-S). The point (1) on the three-

115

dimensional graph is the point where the categories of [C8s] and [D12m] cross. This client's interpretation [D12m] in the context of negative self-definition restricted the possibility of choices of her following behavior selection. The client chose the response K3 as the expression of her negative self image [D12s]. The point (2) on the three-dimensional graph is the point where the categories of [D12m] and [D12s] cross. Next, the client's response (K3, [D12s]) guided the enactment of the doctor (Dr.4). That is, the client's behavior [D12s] affected the choice of doctor's next response of blaming behavior [D12s]. The point (3) on the three-dimensional graph is the point where the categories of [D12s] and [D12s] cross.

Then, the client constructed the meaning of this doctor's utterance (K5, [D12m]) more negatively than before. The point (4) on the three-dimensional graph is the point where the categories of [D12s] and [D12m] cross. This meaning construction (K5, [D12m]) caused the client's next strong complaint (K6, [D12s]) of uncontrollable pain. The point (5) on the three-dimensional graph is the point where the categories of [D12m] and [D12s] cross. Moreover, the doctor's response (Dr.7, [D12s]) to her complaint of the pain was more punitive than the response of Dr.4. The point (6) on the three-dimensional graph is the point where the categories of [D12s] and [D12s] cross. Afterward, this feedback loop was repeated and the same points on the three-dimensional graph were plotted repeatedly.

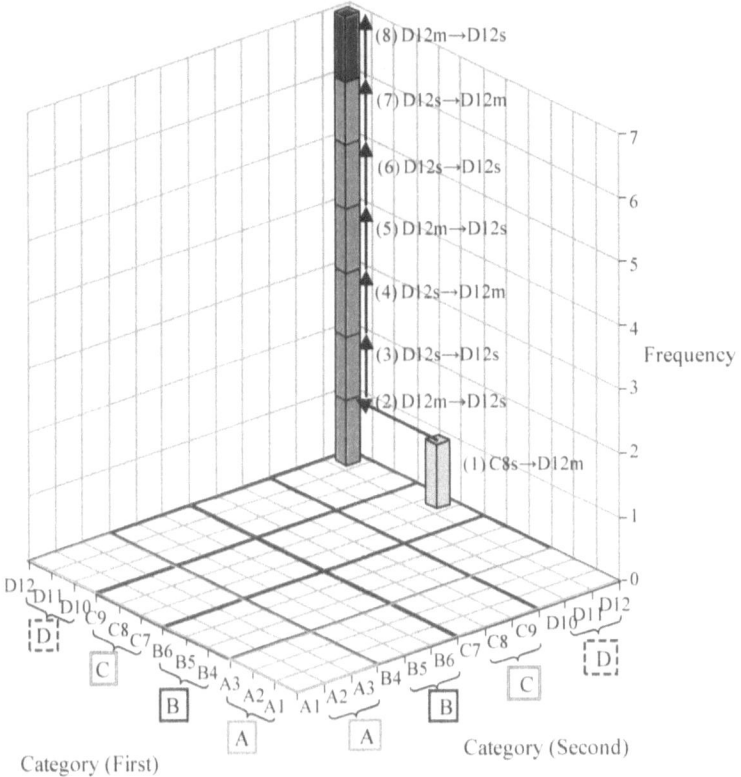

Figure 6.5. The Measurement of the Dynamics of Transaction between Doctor and Client in the Pre-intervention Phase

m: meaning construction, s: relational meaning of utterance,
    A. Social—emotional area: positive reactions
    B. Task area: neutral attempted answers
    C. Task area: neutral questions
    D. Social—emotional area: negative reactions

This figure was modified from Figure3-4 in Oshita (2008). which had been published in K. Kamo and T. Nakaya (eds.). Hyumansarbisu Chosahou wo Manabuhito no Tameni. Kyoto: Sekaishisosha. p. 113.

This vicious cycle occurred whenever the client took medical advice from the doctor in the ward. Without the effective intervention in this process, they will repeat their deviance SpActs with each other as well as the rules which guide the behaviors. The dynamics to generate the negative sequence will be stabilized. As the result, participants can't escape from this suffering world construction game.

If one of these elements in the Figure 6.5. is differentiated, the dynamics of sequence between doctor and client will change and it will cause a change of structure in the dynamics of the client's world construction (Figure 6.4.).

Intervention Strategy

The mechanism of problem amplification is hypothesized as follows: the client's negative reality construction and the deteriorated ability for resolving the pain were reinforced by transactions between the hospital subsystem and office subsystems in her ecological situation (Figure 6.1.). Based on this assessment, the intervention strategy was aimed to intervene in one of the deviance amplifying processes in these subsystems. Moreover, the intervention of this case by the social worker was executed in the context of focusing on the client's ability to control the pain and consistently solve the problem.

The hospital subsystem
In the hospital, the social worker used three tactics to create the dynamics of problem resolution in each of two vicious feedback loops and the deviant transaction between these two loops.

1. The social worker attempted to reconstruct the client's rules of positive reality construction to create a positive life script and escape the vicious cycles by exchanging the level of Episode to the higher level of Relationship which is the reciprocal embeddedness structure shown in Figure 6.4.

2. The social worker intervened in the nurse-client subsystem to create a problem solving feedback loop and strengthen the client's life script that she had the problem resolution ability.

3. The social worker encouraged the client to choose new resolution behavior in transactions with the doctor in the context of newly acquired problem solution behavior. If this were successful, the client who is in the lowest position in Relationship in Figure 6.4. will change into the higher position. According to Figure 6.5., the pinpointed intervention phase was the client's meaning construction and behavior selection response to Dr.1, that is, the connection of the coordinates from (1) to (2).

The office subsystem

The social worker and client designed a practice to seek an improved ability to achieve solution behavior in the social context of the workplace.

Intervention Process

Two intervention steps were taken to improve the client's problem solving ability. The target of the first intervention was the subsystem in the hospital. Her office was targeted for the second intervention.

Creating new rules for her reality construction in the hospital

The intervention process in the hospital was executed in three steps: creation of the client's rules to control the pain, the enforcement of the client's positive rules, and stabilization of client's new reality construction rules in the hospital.

1. Creation of the client's rules to control the pain

The intervention purpose of this step was as shown in Figure 6.6. The symbol $\frac{Ep}{R2}$ indicates that Ep is the higher order context within which relationship 2 is understood (Cronen, Pearce and Tomm, 1985, p. 206). The social worker attempted to help the client reconstruct the relationship 2 in Figure 6.4. between herself and the pain in the context of positive episode constructed through the intervention process.

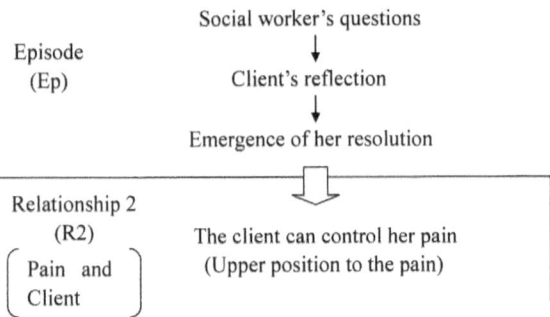

Figure 6.6. The Plan of Transformation Dynamics of Client's Reality Construction

The specific process was as follows: first, in order to minimize the seriousness of her problem and help her to find a simple solution, the social worker recommended that the client record the experiences of pain starting from the phase of the onset of pain, then the phase of increasing pain, and the phase of pain alleviation as a result of receiving the pentazocine of injection everyday for one week. The client was interested in this plan because she had never focused on the former time zone where she receives the pentazocine injection.

In the next session, the client reported the negative results of her practice. The social worker encouraged her to reflect on her behaviors in *the duration* of pain experiences using reflexive circular questions (RCQ; temporal context questions). By using the questions, the client listed the behaviors of the sequence of solution activities for enduring the pain for about *two hours duration* (see pain time zones in Figure 6.7.). The client reported that she attempted to concentrate on watching TV, or reading books to control the pain. Along with these behaviors, the client concentrated on observing the behavior of nurses, and listening for footsteps or the tone of voices of nurses to relieve her pain. These were solution behaviors which she created. However she could not control her pain using these strategies to the point at which she did not need to receive the pentazocine injection.

Following this, the social worker asked the client to reflect on *the frequency* of pain experiences based on her results for one week using the temporal difference questions. The client isolated the painful time as *almost two times in a day*. The client realized that the hours she experienced the pain were two times, approximately both from 21:00 to 24:00 and from 4:00 to 7:00. Through interventions to reflect on the duration of pain experiences, and to differentiate the time zone of a day when the pain appeared, the client identified some long time zones where there was no experience of pain (see Figure 6.7., pain-free time zones). Next, the social worker asked the client to reflect on the solution behaviors for coping with the pain in 'long pain-free time zone' (exploration of exception) using reflexive circular questions (RCQ; temporal context questions). The client answered that talking with other patients or making handicrafts in the hospital ward freed her pain (the emergence of solution behaviors). The client could describe her solution behaviors in which she could be free of pain (i.e., the emergence of new episode).

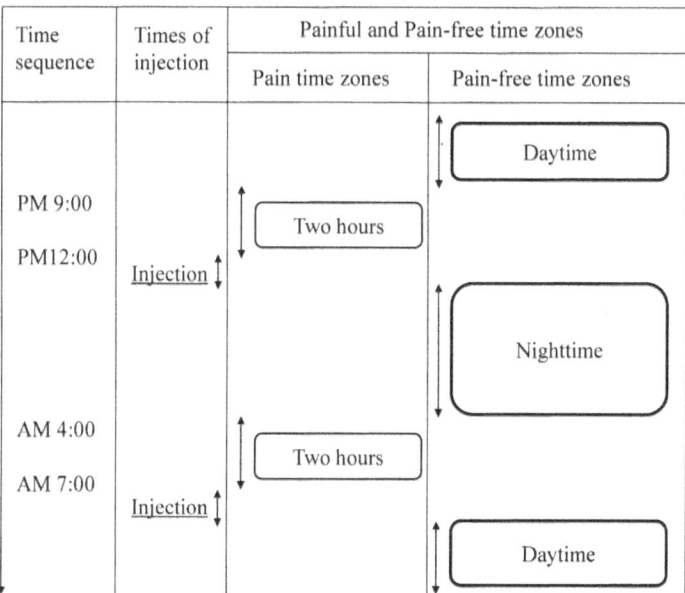

Figure 6.7. The Expansion of Pain-free Hours

The third step in this process was when the social worker encouraged the client to make a plan to help cope with pain all day long. She was helped to enforce the rules of choosing and performing her resolution behavior of coping with the pain using category differences questions. The client remembered the episode of pain control by doing handicrafts and giving them to other patients (emergence of the exception). The client planned to make handicrafts to give them to other patients, especially child patients, as a strategy to control her pain. Afterward, the client made many mascots of the felt owl for the ward staff and other patients. At that time when the client created the handicrafts, she did not feel the pain. Moreover, the people who received the mascot the client made were very delighted and wore it on their clothes, or carried it attached to their bags. Their behaviors had decreased her concentration on the pain. As the result, she could realize that there was *long pain-free time zones* everyday (i.e., the generation of positive episode, relationship and Life script). The client began to gain self-confidence to cope with the pain. Consequently, new reality construction rules with which she could generate a positive self-definition (new Life script), whether or not she had received an injection of pentazocine, were created in this intervention process. These emergences of new episode, relationship and Life script and solution behaviors began to function as a context to solve her problem.

2. The enforcement of the client's rules to control the pain

In the next step, in order to reinforce the client's new rules, the social worker proposed to the chief nurse to consider their approach to the client. The social worker offered to the chief nurse information about the client's ability to control the pain. Nurses in her hospital ward had a meeting and began to change their approaches to the client. Their approach to the client changed to an approach for promoting her ability to endure the pain. They encouraged her attempts to create the mascot as the behavior to control her pain. This new transaction began to occur between nurses and client and the client's paradoxical situation in the hospital subsystem was relieved to some extent. Furthermore, the client's behavior to make an owl mascot was reinforced as the solution behavior, and the experiences of repeated solution behavior began to generate the new client's behavioral rules and meaning construction rules (disappearance of loop 2 in Figure 6.2.). Following the client's success to create the pain control skills, the social worker helped the client to establish the upper position in the transaction between the client and the pain and create the positive self-definition. A new definition of a relationship 2 can create a new life script within the episode as a higher order context.

3. Stabilization of client's new rules of reality construction

In the third step, to trigger the client's new behavior towards the doctor, the social worker asked the client to tell the doctor about her acquisition of new skills to reduce her pain and to offer the doctor the chance to allow her to practice her pain control skills at home. However, the client rejected this advice, because she could not imagine that the doctor would accept this proposal. To change her pessimistic expectation of the doctor's answer, the social worker helped her to imagine the miracle situation where she could persuade the doctor (miracle question). The client answered that she could explain to the doctor the correctness of her opinion only if she would not need the injection any more all day long.

Then, the social worker asked the client to make a small step plan to become a person who need not receive an injection of pentazocine.

Step 1: If I don't feel pain during the morning for three days in duration, I will attempt to leave the hospital for a few hours the following morning to buy material to make handicrafts.

Step 2: If I succeed in achieving this aim, I'll repeat this assignment for three days.

Step 3: If I can clear step 2, I will make an effort to leave the hospital for half a day to clean my house to prepare the leaving hospital for good. This attempt will be repeated two days in a row.

Step 4: If I get over these steps and I don't need to receive the injection all day long, I will attempt to leave the hospital temporarily for one day. I want to attempt it a few times.

Step 5: If I can leave the hospital temporarily for a few days, I will attempt to go to work in the morning.

Through this planning process, the client began to construct the new behavioral (rR) and interpretational rules (cR) which guided her to select solution behaviors and to create a new meaning system. This transformation of rR and cR were the preconditions of the pain control.

In one session after making this plan, the client suddenly reported to the social worker that she had not received an injection for one full day, the previous day (i.e., the occurrence of new Episode and Life script). The report of this successful episode exactly coincided with step 4 in her discharge plan. Subsequently, the social worker evaluated her successful pain control and encouraged her to report these pain control episodes to her doctor.

However, the client insisted that she couldn't carry out the discharge plan because there were a lot of problems besides the pain. The social worker facilitated her reflection on the problems besides the pain. The client explained concretely the two problems; one problem was that she had just started an intravenous treatment, and another problem was that she was insufficiently well to leave the hospital. The client reconstructed the first problem as follows: as the client explained to the social worker that she had to receive an intravenous treatment three times a week, the social worker encouraged the client to reflect on the interval between intravenous treatments. She found more than a one day interval between two treatments.

After the discussion about a particular intravenous treatment, the client continued to insist that the doctor wouldn't accept her problem solving behavior because she believed that the doctor would assess her recent physical wellness condition as insufficient to leave the hospital. The client couldn't expect the doctor's affirmative response to her new utterance selected as the resolution behavior of pain. Her negative construction of a self image was the pre-figurative force which aggravated the difficulty for selecting the resolution behavior. Therefore, to transform the client's pre-figurative force and increase her practical force, the social worker encouraged the client to reflect on the specific situation wherein she would tell the doctor about her ability, using both the reflexive circular question (RCQ) and miracle question. The process was as follows: (SW indicates social worker and CL indicates a client).

1SW: What bothers you about telling the doctor? (RCQ: *categorical contexts*)

2CL: I know it matches my discharge plan, but I don't think the doctor will permit me to leave because I am a long-term in-patient.

3SW: What kind of response do you expect from the doctor, when you report about your ability to control the pain? (RCQ: *temporal contexts and miracle question*)

4CL: He'll be worried and say, "I can't permit you to leave because you don't have enough physical strength right now." If the doctor diagnoses my physical condition in that way, I won't be able to believe that I will have enough physical strength to leave the hospital on my own. Moreover, the weather is too sultry these days, so, I think that if the weather were to become much cooler than now, then I could meet his expectation and would leave the hospital.

5SW: Well, I guess that you are worrying about two things; one is doctor's negative response, and another is that there is no method for dealing with the very sultry weather. Is this right? (RCQ: *category differences*)

6CL: That's right.

7SW: Which problems do you want to cope with first? (RCQ: *category differences*)

8CL: I can't deal with both these problems. Both of them are definitely unchangeable things, I think.

The intervention process from 1SW to 8CL shows the process of minimizing the problem and strengthening her problem solution ability. That is, the social worker identified components of her pre-figuration which foresaw the doctor's negative response and her helplessness in dealing with sultry weather, derived from this pre-figurative force. Based on the assessment mentioned above, the social worker constructed the transformation strategy as follows: if one of constructed meaning is changed, the client's pre-figurative force will be altered and the practical force to improve her ability to leave the hospital temporarily will be strengthened. The priority target of intervention was a way of dealing with the weather.

9SW: Well, ... Shall we at first think about a way of dealing with sultry weather? You worry about the heat, right? If you attempt to leave the hospital temporarily, do you want to change the temperature of any place? (RCQ: *category differences and miracle question*)

10CL: I worry about air conditioning in my house. The air conditioning in my house is not as strong as at the hospital.

11SW: Which rooms in your house do you think need temperature adjustment to best adjust the temperature so as to be the same as the hospital? (RCQ: *category differences*)

12CL: It may be only my bedroom. As my house is situated in the suburbs of the city, the air in my room is cooler than in the hospital.

13SW: Ah, really? What do you worry about, next? (RCQ: *category differences*)

14CL: The next problem is the two hours distance from the hospital to my house.

15SW: What do you worry about on the route from the hospital to your house? (RCQ: *category differences*)

16CL: At first, when I walk from the hospital to the bus stop, and second, while I am waiting on the platform to transfer to the train. I feel hot at that time.

17SW: You feel uncomfortably hot at the bus stop and on the platform . . . . , how long do you have to cope with the sultry weather to go to the bus stop, do you guess? (RCQ: *category differences*)

18CL: It takes five minutes, or so . . . . , I think it is only twenty minutes even if I wait on the platform for the maximum duration.

19SW: Do you think you can cope with twenty minutes of sultry weather, don't you? You are a person who was able to control your severe pain for two hours. Therefore, I believe you can invent some resolution behavior to deal with the twenty minutes of sultry weather (positive reframing). Could you tell me your idea to deal with it? (RCQ: *category differences*)

20CL: I might put on my hat to protect me from the strong sunshine.

21SW: I see, and then? (RCQ: *category differences*)

22CL: I might also bring a cold drink in a plastic bottle.

23SW: Well, that sounds good. You have already had two coping behaviors for the sultry weather. Do you have any more ideas? (RCQ: *category differences*)

24CL: No. I don't have more ideas. Today is a good day to try to temporarily leave the hospital. I really think so. I'll try to ask the doctor to permit my leaving the hospital temporarily from now. I think that I now have the confidence to persuade the doctor to permit my leaving the hospital temporarily.

The intervention process from 9SW to 24CL shows the process of minimizing the problem and an increase of the client's practical ability to select the resolution behavior. The sultry weather was identified as the components of the pre-figurative force that inhibits the generation of resolution behavior. Her resolution behavior to sultry weather was explored by using miracle question, reflexive circular questions (RCQ) and positive reframing. The transformation of this minimized problem became a trigger to identify herself as a person who has the ability to leave the hospital, as well as increasing her solution ability to persuade the doctor. (emergence of new cR). Consequently, she could choose the behavior for telling the doctor her proposal to temporarily leave the hospital (emergence of new rR, selection of her proposal behavior in Figure 6.8.). $\frac{Ep}{R1}$ in Figure 6.8 indicates that Episode is the higher context within which Relationship 1 is understood (Cronen, Pearce and Tomm, 1985, p. 206). The client began to regain confidence to solve her problem by deciding to select the behavior/identity as a controllable person of pain (reinforcement of new Relationship 2).

In fact, the client's new solution behavior caused the doctor's acceptance of her proposal and she could successfully leave the hospital temporarily on that day. A detailed analysis of transforming the transaction between doctor and the client will be shown later. In this way, new rules for a new language game without the complaint of pain began to emerge within the hospital subsystem.

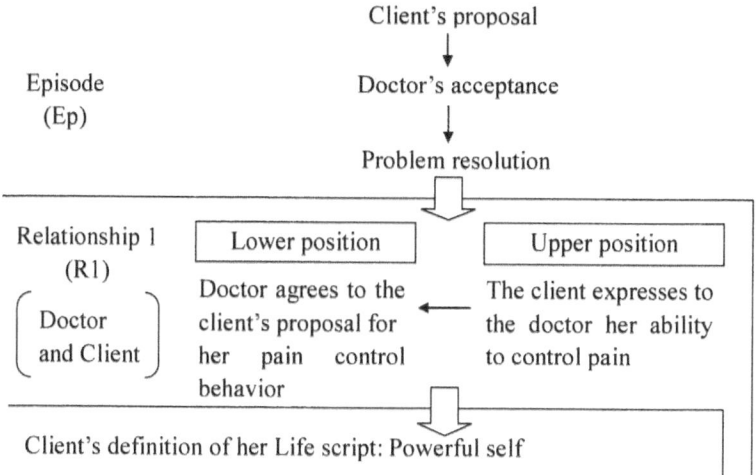

Figure 6.8. Transformation of the Client's Context of Reality Construction

The [Upper position] indicates the subject's position or things in the world which are personified by the client and take a controllable position in his or her circumstance. The [lower position] indicates the subject's position controlled by the other people or personified things.

The extension and stabilization of new rules of the client's reality construction in her ecological system

Although the client succeeded in achieving her goals to temporarily leave the hospital, she kept hesitating to accept her manager's message which required her to come back to office as soon as possible. The client insisted on her returning to the office in perfect condition. The social worker assessed the client's complaint as an expression of the dysfunction in the office subsystem. The client's rejection (Bales' category; D12s) of her manager's message which ordered her to come back to the office as soon as possible generated more coercive orders (Bales' category; D12s). This pattern was the same as the vicious pattern between doctor and client.

Then, to spread the change of the client's cR and rR in the hospital, to her office, a practice plan for adjustment to her office situation was made according to the same small step procedure as the procedure done in her hospital (Figure 6.9.). $\frac{Ep}{R3}$ in Figure 6.9. indicates that Ep is the higher order context within which R3 is understood (Cronen, Pearce and Tomm, 1985, p. 206). The client expresses to the manager her concrete plan to return to the office.

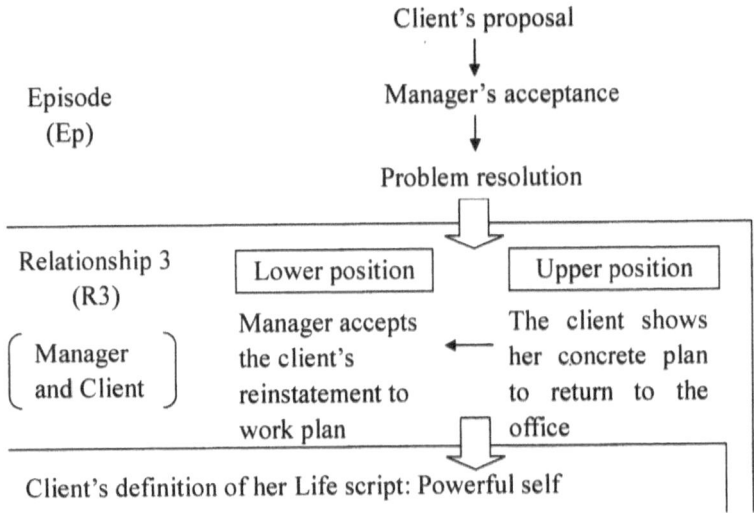

Figure 6.9. Transformation of the Client's Context

The [Upper position] indicates the subject's or objects which are personified by the client and take a controllable position in his or her circumstance. The [lower position] indicates the subject's position controlled by the other people or personified things/objects.

At first, the social worker encouraged her to plan her own program to return to her office using small steps in order to strengthen her self-confidence (cR). The client planned to return to the office for three months on a part-time basis. However, the client expected the negative response of office manager against the program she made. Therefore, the social worker encouraged the client to think about the choice of a specific resolution behavior (rR) to the expected negative response of the office manager in the new context of her practical force constructed in the hospital subsystem. As she explained it to the social worker, the client constructed her plan to return to the office from setting aside only two hours for work in the morning. This is the problem resolution method using small steps which she learned in her hospital (Bales' category; B4s). Fortunately, the client succeeded in persuading the manager to initiate her own plan to return to the office. Consequently, the vicious feedback loop 3 (Figure 6.3.) disappeared. That is, the rules of problem resolution in the hospital subsystem were applied in the office subsystem, as well, and the client practiced her problem resolution behavior effectively.

Results

The transformation of the transaction between doctor and client was clarified after discussing her attempt to get permission to temporarily leave the hospital. Subsequently, the social worker required the client to reflect on her attempt to get permission. The client answered that it was most effective to keep insisting on her proposal against the doctor's opposition. The data of this transaction was gathered by using the tracking interviewing skills (DCQ), and they were categorized based on Bales' categories as shown in Table 6.2. In Table 6.2., 's' stands for relational meaning of utterance, and 'm' is the symbol for meaning construction. The number from (1') to (9') in Table 6.2. indicates the point on the three-dimensional graph in Figure 6.10.

Table 6.2. Categorized Assessment Data of Post-intervention

Subject	The elements of sequence	Categorization	
Dr.1	How about your condition, today?	C8s	(1')
K2	The doctor asked me to evaluate my condition	C8m	(2')
K3	I want to leave the hospital temporarily	B4s	(3')
Dr.4	I can't permit your temporarily leaving the hospital as long as you are receiving the intravenous treatment	D12s	(4')
K5	The doctor disagreed that she could temporarily leave the hospital	D10m	(5')
K6	Could you stop the intravenous treatment because I want to try from now soon?	B4s	(6')
Dr.7	I don't want to permit your temporarily leaving the hospital until the effect of the intravenous treatment is clarified, speaking honestly	B5s	(7')
K8	The doctor presented me with a condition for temporarily leaving the hospital	B5m	(8')
K9	What do you think about leaving the hospital temporarily during the interval between intravenous-treatments ?	B4s	(9')
Dr.10	It is an acceptable condition. I permit you to temporarily leave the hospital	A3s	

Note. m: meaning construction, s: relational meaning of utterance, Dr.: doctor, K: client.

Table 6.2 was translated and modified from Table 3-6 in Oshita, Y. (2008). Shakaikouseishugiteki Kouka Sokuteihou no Jissai. In K. Kamo and T. Nakaya (eds.). Hyumansarbisu Chosahou wo Manabuhito no Tameni. Kyoto: Sekaishisosha. p. 128.

The number of categories of relational meaning of utterances (s) and meaning construction (m) increased greatly in Table 6.2. compared with Table 6.1. The client's meaning construction of Dr.1 was changed from D12m to C8m, according to Bales' category. This meaning construction (K2) guided her next choice of behavior (K3) of B4s. Although the doctor's response (Dr.4) to client's utterance has a negative feeling, the client's meaning construction (K5) of the doctor's response is classified into D10m, whose level of anger was lower than D12m. Then, the client could select the solution behavior (B4s) successively (K6). This client's repeated selection of B4s became a force to bring out the doctor's next response of B5s (Dr.7). The client was able to select positive meaning construction (K8) against the next response of the doctor. This positive meaning construction (B5m) reinforced the following resolution behavior of B4s (K9). In this process, the dynamics of the language game played by the client and the doctor transformed from the contradiction amplifying pattern, to the problem solution pattern, and the client's social adaptation level began to improve.

Each message in this sequence is categorized according to the Bales' interaction analysis frame which was explained in Appendix B in detail. The Table 6.2. shows the dynamics of the sequence of messages. These categorized data in Table 6.2. are plotted on a three-dimensional graph represented in Figure 6.10. The specific procedure for making a three-dimensional graph is the same as the procedure shown in Figure 6.5.

In the pre-intervention phase, the client's choice of behavior and meaning construction moves from (1) (C8s, D12m) to (2) (D12m, D12s) as shown in Table 6.1. and Figure 6.5. In the post-intervention phase, the sequence of transaction moves from (1') (C8s, C8m) to (2') (C8m, B4s) in Table 6.2. and Figure 6.10. This difference of dynamics of problem solving activity is clear among these two phases and the problem solving ability of the client is obviously improved in the latter phase represented in Table 6.2. and Figure 6.10. from (3') to (9'). This transformation of the dynamics indicates the disappearance of loop 1 in Figure 6.2.

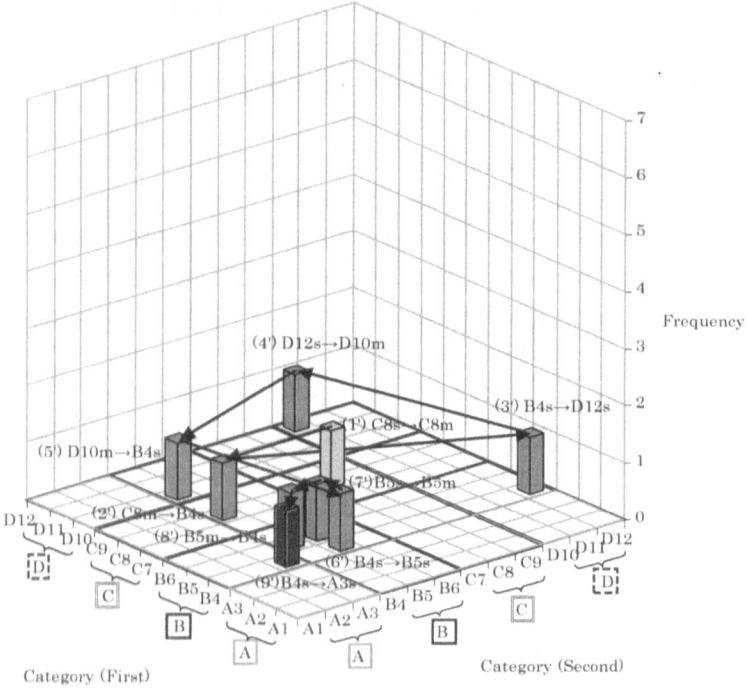

Figure 6.10. The Measurement of the Changed Dynamics of Transaction between Doctor and Client in the Post-intervention Phase

m: meaning construction, s: relational meaning of utterance,
   A. Social—emotional area: positive reactions
   B. Task area: neutral attempted answers
   C. Task area: neutral questions
   D. Social—emotional area: negative reactions
This figure was modified from Figure3-8 in Oshita (2008). which had been published in K. Kamo and T. Nakaya (eds.). Hyumansarbisu Chosahou wo Manabuhito no Tameni. Kyoto: Sekaishisosha. p. 131.

The disappearance of DAFL in the hospital subsystem means the solution of the problem obstructing the client's leaving the hospital. After leaving the hospital, according to the reinstatement plan the client had designed, she returned to the office. The client persuaded the manager to accept the reinstatement plan she had designed. Thus, after being discharged and returned to the office, she did not complain of pain at all. Consequently, the language game of her pain which controlled the ecological system was over.

Conclusion

The effectiveness of the new social work practice model based on the theory of language game and CMM was shown in the proceeding case analysis of pain complaints. That is, the complaint of pain was defined in terms of speech acts which were guided by cR and rR in the interpersonal transactional process. Therefore, the strategy to intervene in this case of the pain complaint was defined as the transformation of the language game which is directed by the rule to keep the pain complaining behavior.

At first, the client found the solution behavior to control her pain through the social worker's intervention. Her discovery of a new solution to cope with the pain involved changing the rules of speech acts in the transaction between the doctor and the client. She could clearly explain to the doctor the discovery of the method to control her pain. Her explanation of pain control method changed the doctor's prescription for her. The doctor accepted the client's explanation and permitted her temporarily leaving the hospital. The social worker helped her to identify the newly acquired problem solution skill used in the transaction between the doctor and the client to get the permission to temporarily leave the hospital. The problem solving skills which the client identified with the social worker's intervention involved differentiating the problem, finding minimalist solution behaviors, enabling the acquisition of a meta-level position to reconstruct her reality. These new skills were used to explain her plan to return to her office. As a result, the client's long-term hospitalization ended, and she accomplished a return to the office by using the series of skills of circular questioning and SFBT based on MCMM.

Yumi Oshita, PhD, and Kiyoshi Kamo, MSW

The effectiveness usage of the measurement model mentioned in Chapter 3 of PART 1 was shown through this specific case study. The elements of a transactional process between doctor and client that are one of DAFL in the client's ecological system were categorized by using Bales' category of interactional analysis (see Appendix B: The Bales system of categories used in observation). By visualizing the changing process of elements in the transaction sequence categorized in the three-dimensional graph, the dynamics of intervention in the transaction between doctor and client was accurately assessed and the change of the dynamics between pre-intervention and post-intervention in doctor-client subsystem as a result of strength intervention was clarified.

Acknowledgement

We would like to express gratitude to our client who was willing to agree to the presentation of her case in this study.

EPILOGUE

TOWARD THE CREATION OF A NEW APPROACH TO SOCIAL WORK

Uniqueness and Weaknesses of Our Approach

In this epilogue, we'll first explain the originality of our approach of social work, and then briefly discuss its possible weaknesses. In this book we present a new approach to social work from a social constructionist perspective. This is an example of a paradigm shift in social work practice. Up until now, we have rarely found theoretical approaches to social work from such a radically new perspective. As we begin such consideration of the new social work paradigm, many logical problems appear. To solve the problems in our approach, continuing research in theory and practice is needed. This work is a study examining themes of social theories, skills, and measuring intervention effects. A thorough examination of the themes is not easy. Another book will be required to fully explicate and develop these themes and results in a comprehensive way.

Uniqueness of Our Approach

The concept of social work of our approach
What is social work? In Japan, the answer is unclear, and because of this, there is great confusion in this field. For example, many of our graduate school students have reported on the disastrous

situation which social workers in Japan face. They have reported that a lot of social workers experience burnout in Japan, because they have to help a wide variety of clients without the benefit of a consistently effective method. Their descriptions of the problems which social workers in Japan face have impressed us and motivated us to closely review academic publications of social work in recent years. We did a thorough review of many academic journals and other social work publications. We reached the conclusion that the theories and the skills of current social work are stuck in a blind alley. This conclusion is what motivated us ten years ago to embark on the theorization of a new social work approach. Thus we began a re-construction of the social work approach with consideration of the basic social theory, skills, and empirical measurement. The foundation we have developed is an elucidation of a concept of the social world and concepts of social work which are intended to form the main components of an adequate social work theory.

Social theory and the social constructionist approach

Generally speaking, social work is defined as theories and skill set for interpersonal transformation. Therefore when we define social work, we must articulate a theoretical model which can adequately account for the process of social and psychological transformation which lies at the heart of our approach. Traditional Marxism is a typical macro social theory which prophesies the direction of stages of social development and prescribes a method for transformation of the social system. However, the Marxist paradigm is too rigid and inflexible to be useful for real life situations of social flux. The social theory we need is not historical prophecy. We need a theory which explains a rapid change and the structure of transactions in daily life.

Our social theory was composed by modifying Coordinated Management of Meaning (CMM) theory (Cronen and Pearce, 1985) which is the theoretical framework to explain the radical transformation of the social world. Our modified CMM (MCMM) explains the structuralizing process of the social world as the dynamics between embedded levels of contexts and the dynamic of behavior selection. This MCMM theory denies the existence of the objective world and emphasizes the subjective process of the structure of social worlds. Therefore some social theorists may point to a similarity between social construction of reality theory (Berger and Luckmann, 1970) and our social theory. Berger and Luckmann assume that the social world is not an objective real world but is rather constituted through transaction using symbols. Although we can find a similarity between Berger's and Luckmann's social theory and ours, we have to clear points of difference, as well. Their social theory presupposes consensus in the process of social world construction. In contrast, social theory based on MCMM is a dialectical one which explains the radical changes of social worlds by focusing on the dynamics between embedded levels of meaning (Cronen, Pearce, and Tomm, 1985).

In addition, we'll also describe how our approach is different from a social work approach based on narrative theory (White and Epston, 1990). To explain social transformation, our approach analyzes the dynamic relationship between the life situation at a micro level where transaction develops, and the macro level social system which forms the structure of behavior rules and meaning construction rules. In contrast, advocates of the narrative approach maintain that a dominant story constructs the person and social world; the narrative theorist reifies narrative, and explains a construction of social reality using the concept of the generation power of the linear narrative. The problems with this approach are (1) reification of narrative, and (2) adoption of a linear causality.

The concept of work as a practice to improve client's problem solving skills of our approach

What is the work? Conventional psychotherapy presupposes the existence of pathology in the psychological world. Then psycho-social therapy tries to find a past cause for the pathology and remove it, based on this ontological position. However, we reject the presupposition of the existence of an objective pathology in the inner psychological world, as well as the linear explanation of appearance of pathology. We encourage the client to discover the solution of psycho-social problems by using various skills; our practice based on MCMM is accomplished by using the circular question skill which is the technique for producing a difference of meaning construction and behavior selection in the transactional world and adding the Solution Focused Brief Therapy (SFBT) techniques which are used to identify present and future solutions. For example, we try realizing the past potential problem solving story using the circular questions of the Calgary school. In this approach, we differentiate the current suffering story of the client, and draw out the client's solution skills by helping him or her reflexively examine this story. Moreover, we help the client to visualize a success scene in the future so that he or she may discover the new solution skills using the SFBT techniques. This solution oriented practice using both differentiation questions and SFBT techniques is the feature of our practice.

As our practice model deals with the behavior and cognition of the client, many social workers often misunderstand our social constructionist approach as being the same as the cognitive-behavioral approach. There is the clear difference between the cognitive-behavioral approach and our social constructionist approach. The cognitive-behavioral social work approach adopts a linear causal framework and seeks to remove causes which have created ostensibly pathological behavior and problematic cognition (Thomlison, and Thomlison, 1996, pp. 139-168). However, our social constructionist approach denies both this linear causality and perspective on pathology. We value the problem solving ability which client inherently possesses. To draw out this problem solving ability, the social worker questions the client to elicit the solution method which he or she holds in potential.

The methodology of measurement of results

The intervention effect has to be measured to show the usefulness of the approach. The cognitive-behavioral approach compares the incidence of pathological behavior or recognition between pre- and post-intervention. This measuring method is excellent for quantitative comparison of limited variables, but has a weak point. It cannot measure the transformation process of a transaction. Our measurement method can compare the transformation process between pre- and post-intervention. We designed this methodology to quantify qualitative transactional data of these intervention effects, based on Bales' frame of interaction analysis. However, Bales framework did not deal with the element of meaning construction in the interaction. Unlike Bales, our approach includes both behavior and meaning constructions. Therefore our research is an original application of his model to real therapeutic interactions.

The Weakness of Our Approach

We collected social constructionist theories from Wittgenstein (1953), Bateson (1972, 1979), Watzlawick, Weakland and Fisch (1974), Cronen and Pearce (1985) to de Shazer and Dolan (2006). We chose particularly useful concepts from those writings. Then we combined these concepts and constructed a paradigm for social work practice. As the purpose of our discussion is the construction of a new theory for social work practice, the understanding of these original theories was superficial and the method of integration of these concepts and theorization was somewhat arbitrary. As a result, some logical contradictions remain in our approach. The most serious problem concerns the generation of difference.

The solution focused social worker assumes that the problem is constructed by the autonomous client. Therefore, the problem solving practice begins from the intervention, to encourage the client to differentiate the old problem definition in a form that can be solved. Moreover the social worker expects the client to differentiate his or her old problem solution behaviors. The essential feature of our approach is the generation of difference in the client's behavior selection and meaning construction. This practice presupposes the possibility of an infinite differentiation of the problem solving activities in real life. However in real life there are certain cases where this is practically impossible. If the movement of differentiation stops for the client, this theoretical practice can't stand up. Can the client keep infinitely giving a new meaning to the world and look for new solution behaviors? For instance, we can ask as follows; how can the patient with a heavy dementia continuously differentiate his or her world? Up to now, the solution focused social worker has not sufficiently presented a systematic answer to this question. This solution focused practice has to clarify the intervention method for the particular situation. There are some circumstances in which there is a decline in the ability of the client to find any useful differentiation.

Moreover, the number of cases is insufficient to prove the effectiveness of our approach. More intensive case studies are needed to prove its theoretical and practical superiority to other approaches.

Conclusion

The main purpose of this work was to clarify the theoretical preconditions which prove that social work is a practical science. The social worker has to clearly define the basic theory, the techniques, and the measurement method so that it may establish itself as a practical science. We presented an example of the theoretical application of a new approach. The traditional social work practitioner may hesitate to examine their presuppositions and re-construct a new practice, because such examination is a purely theoretical affair, and may seem to be unrelated to practice activity. However, if we abandon the effort of finding a new theorization, social work will not be able to survive. We hope that our discussion about the social work practice from a social constructionist view point will stimulate new theoretical growth for social work practice.

Yumi Oshita
Kiyoshi Kamo

APPENDICES

Appendix A: Framework for Assessment, Intervention and Measurement of Social Work Models

Kiyoshi Kamo and Yumi Oshita

The Characteristics of Assessment and Intervention

The Assessment Procedure of Five Social Work Models

The Circular Questions Model and the Solution Focused Skills Model share a common assessment procedure. A client presents a suffering story. The client's suffering story is transformed into a system of episodes by the social worker using the descriptive circular questions (DCQ). The episode which is described by the client as the most difficult to solve is converted into a sequence of elements of act selection (s) and meaning construction (m) by the social worker using DCQ. What is wholly original in our approach is a theoretical framework for social work practice which explains speech acts not only from the viewpoint of the receiver's meaning construction, but from the point of view of the sender's utterance selection. Then the dynamics of the sequence is assessed.

The categorical distinction between DCQ and RCQ (reflexive circular questions) depends on the social workers' intention when they use these questions (Tomm, 1985, p. 35).

The assessments of the Positive Reframing Model are categorized into two groups. The first assessment group of the Positive Reframing Model is applied to persons who have an ability to explain the problematic situation verbally. The assessment procedure of the first group is the same as the assessment procedure of the Circular Questions Model and the Solution Focused Skills Model above mentioned. The second assessment group of the Positive Reframing Model is applied for persons who do not have enough verbalizing skills of communication. The assessment procedure of the second group focuses on three components of the clients' life situation, which consists of their behaviors, their verbal communication, and the structured physical world as constructed by the clients' activities.

The assessment procedure of the Paradoxical Model is simple. The social worker simply encourages the clients to describe the negative episode in their life situation in order to find the effective paradoxical prescription method.

Circular questions model
Intervention phase 1

After the above mentioned assessment, the client reflects on the sequence of act selection (s) and the meaning construction (m). He or she finds the problem solution method by differentiating 's' or 'm' by the social worker's reflexive circular questions (RCQ).

Intervention phase 2

Here, a client practices new 's' or 'm' which he or she differentiated from the old 's' or 'm' with the help of social worker in his or her life situation.

Intervention phase 3

A client reports the result of his or her practice to the social worker. The social worker next helps him or her to describe the sequence of the practice by DCQ. Moreover, the social worker helps the client to examine the sequence of the practice by RCQ.

Generation of a new story

The client constructs a new problem solving episode which is composed of the new 's' or 'm' by the social worker's intervention using reflexive circular questions (RCQ). This new problem solving skill becomes integrated as a new life skill. The social worker helps the client to extend the dynamics of the re-constructed episode across the client's life situation, and encourages him or her to structure each new episode. The client realizes a new structure for a meaningful life world.

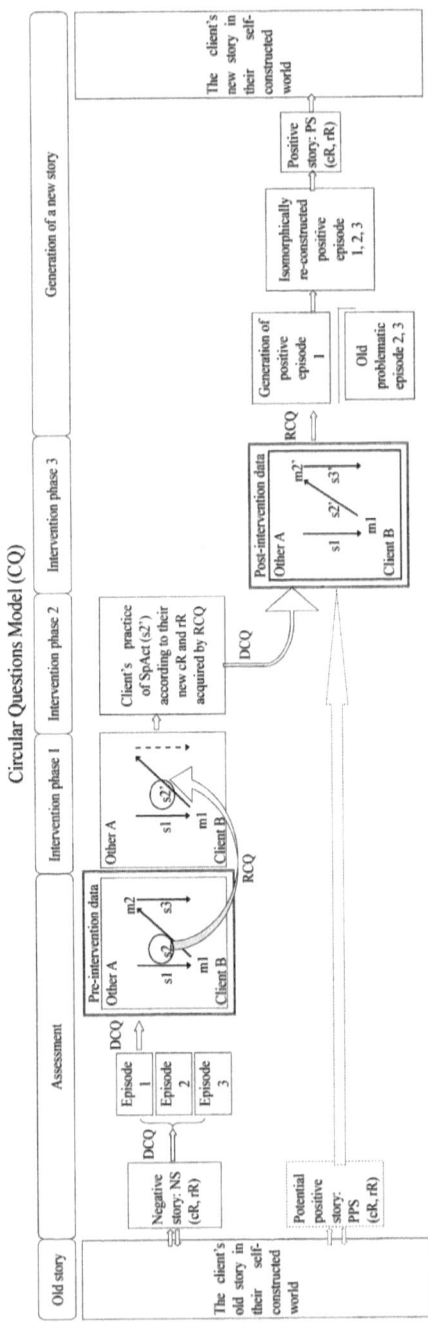

Note. DCQ: descriptive circular questions, RCQ: reflexive circular questions, cR: Constitutive rules, rR: Regulative rules, SpAct (m, s): speech act (meaning construction, act), ⟹ : for social worker's intervention skills

Solution focused skills model

After the assessment of the client's description of episodes, the social worker helps the client to visualize the method of problem solution using the solution focused skills of miracle question and questions of exceptions.

<u>Intervention phase 1</u>

A client converts the story of the problem solution into the chain of the action and the meaning construction by the social worker's DCQ.

<u>Intervention phase 2</u>

Then client practices the solution story sequence.

<u>Intervention phase 3</u>

The social worker helps the client to describe the practice of the solution story by DCQ. Then the social worker encourages the client to examine the practice of their newly constructed sequence of the problem solving activities using RCQ.

<u>Generation of a new story</u>

The social worker helps the client to extend the dynamics of the re-constructed episode across the client's life situation, and encourages him or her to structure each new episode. The client realizes a new structure for a meaningful life world.

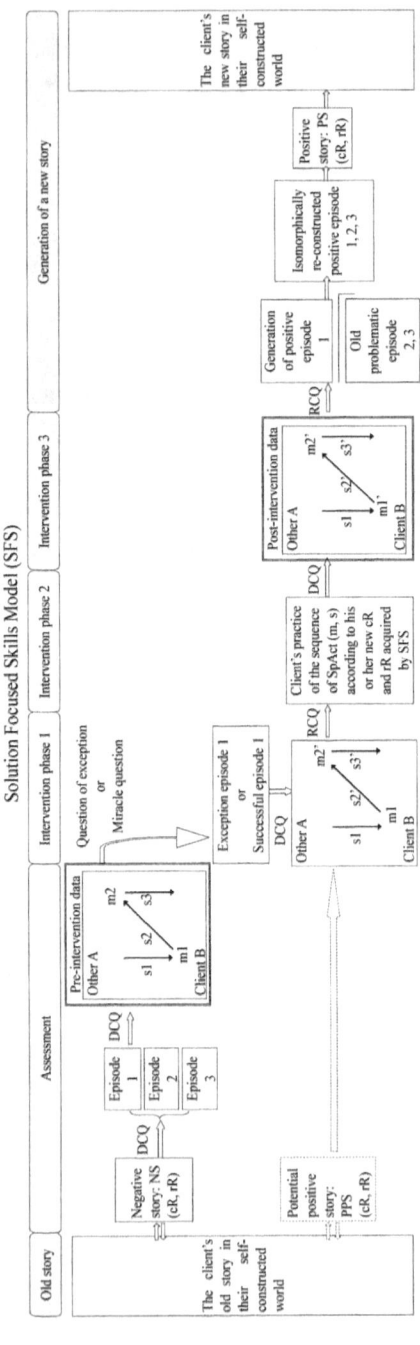

Note. DCQ: descriptive circular questions, RCQ: reflexive circular questions, cR: Constitutive rules, rR: Regulative rules, SpAct (m, s): speech act (meaning construction, act), ⟹ : for social worker's intervention skills

Positive reframing model 1

<u>Intervention phase 1</u>

After the client's description of the problematic episode, this episode is positively reframed by the social worker. The social worker helps the client to change this reframed episode to the sequence of the utterances and meaning construction of other's utterances. The social worker gives a client a chance to refine the behavior selection of positively reframed episode using RCQ. The refined behavior selections are positively reframed by the social worker and then the social worker prescribes these behaviors for the client.

<u>Intervention phase 2</u>

If the client accepts the practice of positively reframing episode, he or she practices the skill of positively creative reframing acts and meaning construction.

<u>Intervention phase 3</u>

The result of the practice is described by DCQ. Then the described new episode is reframed by the social worker's positive reframing skill. Then, using the social worker's RCQ, the client is able to reflect the positively reframed episode.

<u>Generation of a new story</u>

The social worker helps the client to extend the dynamics of the re-constructed episode across their life situation, and encourages him or her to structure each new episode. The client realizes a new structure for a meaningful life world.

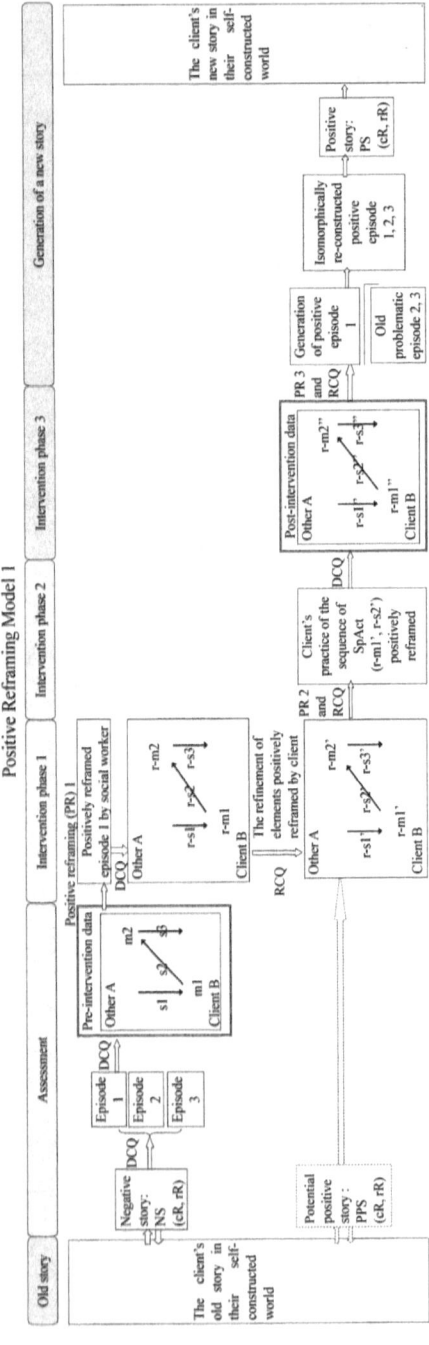

Note. DCQ: descriptive circular questions, RCQ: reflexive circular questions, cR: Constitutive rules, rR: Regulative rules, SpAct (m, s): speech act (meaning construction, act), ⟹ : for social worker's intervention skills

Positive reframing model 2

<u>Intervention phase 1</u>

The social worker uses the positive reframing skill to change the negative recognition framework of the client to a positive one, which will then fit his or her life situation. Through the social worker's DCQ, if the client accepts the social worker's positive reframing, the client is helped to describe each structure of (1), (2), and (3). Through the social worker's use of RCQ, the client can differentiate each of the basic elements of his or her episode, and convert the basic elements into a new non-verbal and verbal problem solution schema. This client's construction of a new solution schema is reframed positively by the social worker again, and the social worker prescribes the practice of a new acquired skill.

<u>Intervention phase 2</u>

The client practices the new prescribed problem solution schema.

<u>Intervention phase 3</u>

The social worker's DCQ helps the client to verbally or non-verbally describe his or her practice of the new solution schema. The social worker positively reframes the client's description of solution activities to confirm his or her ability. The client is motivated to reflect the results of his or her practice through the social worker's RCQ.

<u>Generation of a new story</u>

The social worker helps the client to extend the dynamics of the re-constructed episode across the client's life situation, and encourages him or her to structure each new episode. The client realizes a new structure for a meaningful life world.

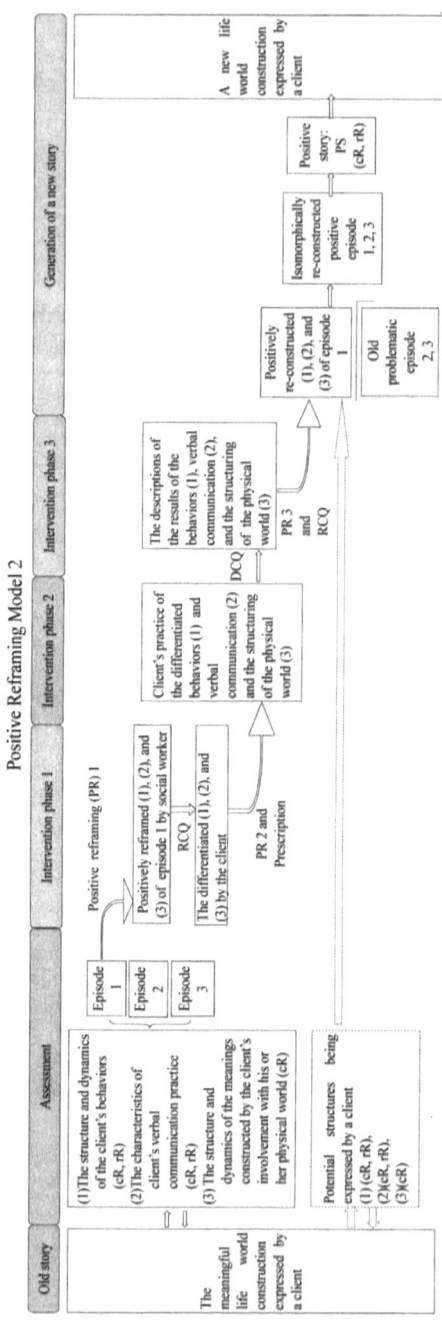

Note. DCQ: descriptive circular questions, RCQ: reflexive circular questions, cR: Constitutive rules, rR: Regulative rules, ⟹ : for social worker's intervention skills

Paradoxical model

The social worker actualizes the problematic sequential data by DCQ.

Intervention phase 1

This sequential data is positively reframed through the social worker's positive reframing skill.

Intervention phase 2

After the positive reframing, the client is prescribed to use these new positively reframed problematic behaviors.

Generation of a new story

Traditional intervention strategies aim at changing the cause of the problem. Contrary to this, paradoxical intervention abandons the concept of the causal relationship and prescribes the practice of the problematic behaviors. If the client refuses to follow this prescription, the opportunity to deal with the problematic episode disappears. Even if the client accepts the prescription, the client's problem also disappears. If the positive reframing explanation is insufficient, and the validity of the prescription of the positive reframing is not persuasive enough for the client, the problematic transaction will continue.

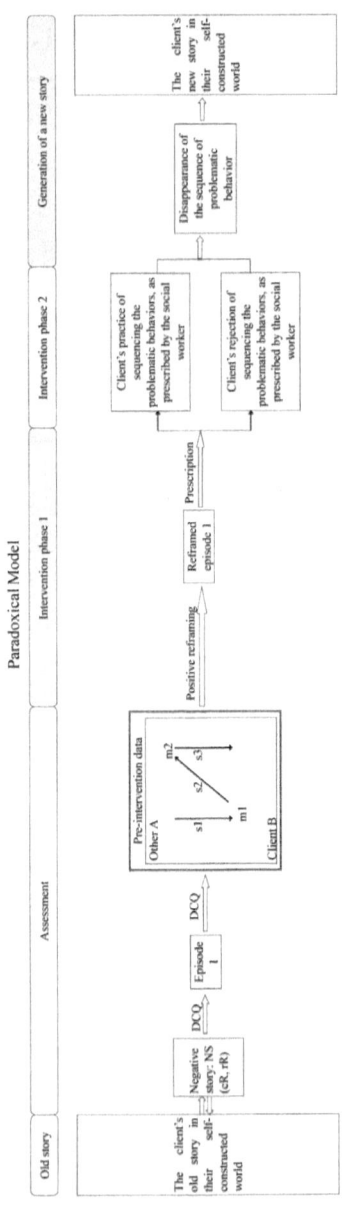

Note. DCQ: descriptive circular questions, RCQ: reflexive circular questions, cR: Constitutive rules, rR: Regulative rules, SpAct (m, s): speech act (meaning construction, act), ⟹ : for social worker's intervention skills

In many cases, it is rare that these intervention models are used independently; they can be effectively used together.

Appendix B: Measurement Method of Intervention Effect

Yumi Oshita and Kiyoshi Kamo

The Procedure for Measurement

The elements of the sequence in the pre-intervention and the post-intervention phases are categorized according to Bales' interaction analysis framework. The categorized data are then plotted on a three-dimensional graph, and pre-intervention and post-intervention phase data are compared.

The Bales System of Categories Used in Observations

A. Social- emotional area: positive reactions
  1. Shows solidarity, raises other's status, gives help, rewards
  2. Shows tension release, jokes, laughs, shows satisfaction
  3. Agrees, shows passive acceptance, understands, concurs, complies
B. Task area: neutral attempted answers
  4. Gives suggestion, direction, implying autonomy for others
  5. Gives opinion, evaluation, analysis, expresses feelings, wish
  6. Gives orientation, information, repeats, clarifies, confirms
C. Task area: neutral questions
  7. Asks for orientation, information, repetition, confirmation
  8. Asks for opinion, evaluation, analysis, expression of feeling
  9. Asks for suggestion, direction, possible ways of action
D. Social- emotional area: negative reactions
  10. Disagrees, shows passive rejection, formality, withholds resources
  11. Shows tension increase, asks for help, withdraws out of field
  12. Shows antagonism, deflates other's status, defends or asserts self

(Bales, 1950)

157

Categorizing the tracking data

Each element of behavior selection (s) is categorized depending on the description of the subject's meaning of his or her act. On the other hand, each element of meaning construction (m) is also categorized depending on the other person's meaning construction in relation to the subject's behavior selection. For example, X said to Y, "Z always acted up while he was eating. I wonder how to deal with this problem." (see Table 3.2. of PART 1) This act was selected by X to ask for Y's opinion. Therefore, the element 'X1' is categorized to C7 according to Bales' category; Y described 'X1' as meaning that X needs some information to deal with their son. Consequently, Y's meaning construction or interpretation of X1 is categorized at C7.

Plotting the tracking data

The first element and the second element in the tracking data are plotted, first. For example, according to Table 3.2. of PART 1), the first element is X's behavior selection and the second is Y's meaning construction. Therefore, the plotting starts from (1) C7s→C7m (Plotting step 1).

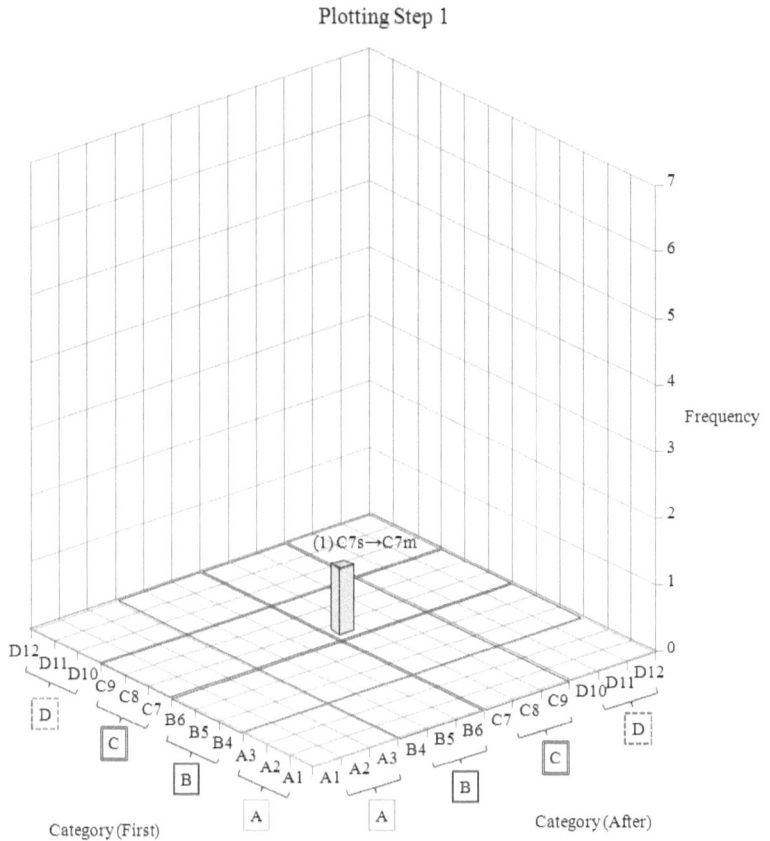

Plotting Step 1

Secondly, Y's behavior is chosen based on Y's meaning construction to X1. Therefore, the next plotting point is (2) C7m→B6s (Plotting step 2).

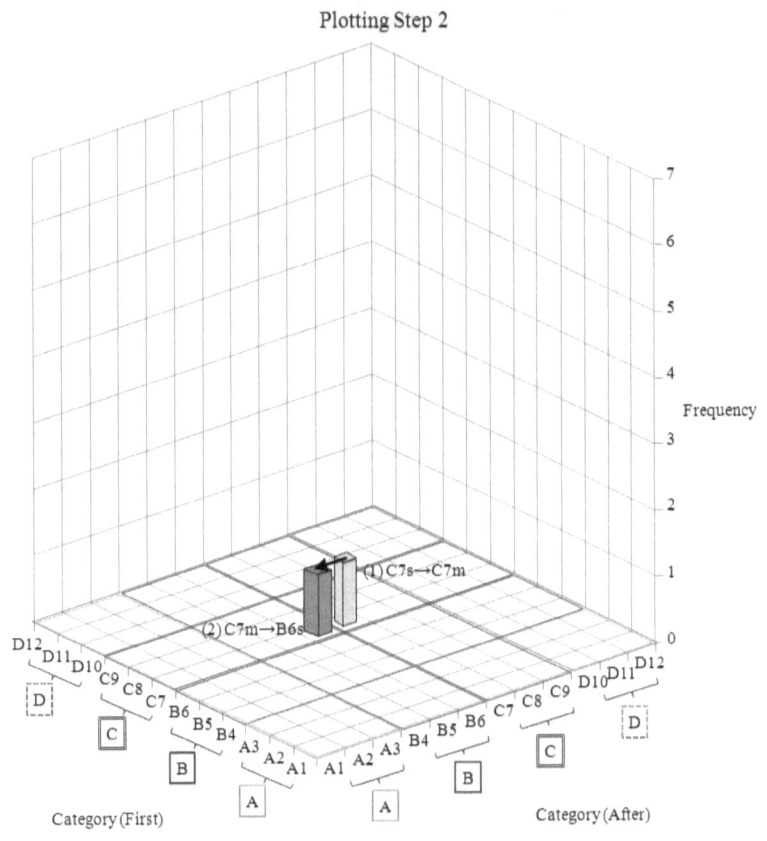

Plotting Step 2

Then, Y's behavior (B6s) is constructed by X; X's meaning construction is B6 according to Table 3.2. of PART 1. Therefore, the third plotting point is (3) B6s→B6m (Plotting step 3).

Plotting Step 3

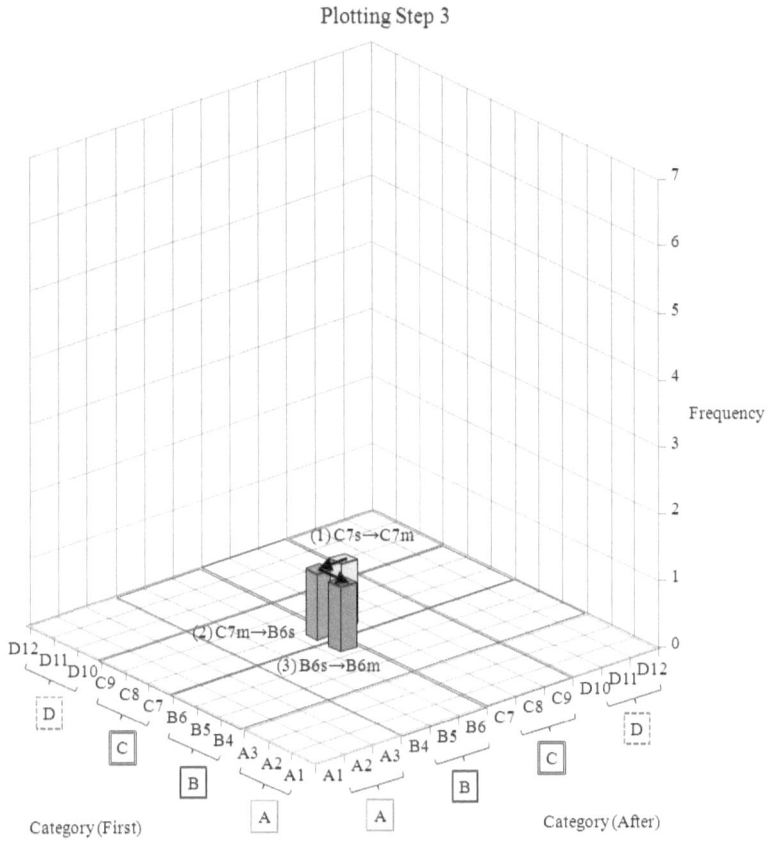

The tracking data from the beginning to the end are plotted in turn on the three-dimensional graph. The completed three-dimensional graph is shown in Chapter 3 of PART 1. A graph of the other case is shown in Chapter 6 of PART 2.

REFERENCE

Anderson, H. (1997). *Conversation, Language, and Possibilities: A Postmodern Approach to Therapy.* New York: Basic Books.

Bales, R. F. (1950). *Interaction Process Analysis: A Method for the Study of Small Groups.* Cambridge, Mass: Addison-Wesley Press, Inc.

Bateson, G. (1972). *Steps to an Ecology of Mind.* New York: Ballantine.

Bateson, G. (1979). *Mind and Nature: A Necessary Unity.* Toronto: Bantam Books, Inc.

Berger, P. L., and Luckmann, T. (1966). *The Social Construction of Reality: A Treatise in the Sociology of Knowledge.* Garden City: Doubleday.

Bertalanffy, L. V. (1968). *General Systems Theory.* New York: Baziller.

Biestek, F. P. (1957). *The Casework Relationship.* Chicago, Illinois: Loyola University Press.

Connie, E., and Metcalf, E. (eds.). (2009). *The Art of Solution Focused Therapy.* New York: Springer Publishing Company.

Constantine, L. L. (1986). *Family Paradigms: The Practice of Theory in Family Therapy.* New York: Guilford Press.

Corcoran, J. (2003). Solution-Focused Therapy with Oppositional Defiant Disorder. In J. Corcoran (ed.). *Clinical Applications of Evidence-Based Family Interventions*. Oxford: Oxford University Press.

Cronen, V. E., and Pearce, W. B. (1985). Toward an Explanation of How the Milan Method Works: An Invitation to a Systemic Epistemology and the Evolution of Family Systems. In D. Campbell and R. Draper (eds.). *Applications of Systemic Family Therapy: The Milan Approach* (pp. 69-84). New York: Grune and Stratton.

Cronen, V. E., Pearce, W. B., and Tomm, K. (1985). A Dialectical View of Personal Change. In K. J. Gergen and K. E. Davis (eds.). *The Social Construction of the Person* (pp. 203-224). New York: Springer-Verlag.

De Jong, P., and Berg, I. K. (2002). *Interviewing for Solution: Second Edition*. Australia: Brooks/Cole.

de Shazer, S., and Dolan, Y. (eds.). (2006). *More Than Miracles: The State of Art of Solution Focused Brief Therapy*. New York: The Haworth Press, Inc.

Gergen, K. J. (1985). Social Constructionist Inquiry: Context and Implications. In K. J. Gergen and K. E. Davis (eds.). *The Social Construction of the Person* (pp. 3-18). New York: Springer-Verlag.

Gergen, K., and Kaye, J. (1992). Beyond Narrative in the Negotiation of Therapeutic Meaning. In S. McNamee and K. J. Gergen (eds.). *Therapy as Social Construction* (pp. 166-185). London: Sage Publications.

Hartman, A., and Laird, J. (1983). *Family-Centered Social Work Practice*. New York: Free Press.

Hoffman, L. (1981). *Foundations of Family Therapy: A Conceptual Framework for Systems Change*. New York: Basic Books.

Hoffman, L. (1992). A Reflexive Stance for Family Therapy. In S. McNamee and K. J. Gergen (eds.). *Therapy as Social Construction* (pp. 7-24). London: Sage Publications.

Hudson, W. W. (1978). First Axioms of Treatment, *Social Work, 1,* 65-66.

Kamo, K., Maeda, K., and Oshita, Y. (2006). Jidouyougoshisetsu de Kurasu Higyakutaijido e no Shoguhou (Social Work Practice for the Abused Child at a Residential Care Institution for Children). In K. Kamo (ed.). *Higyakutaijido e no Shienron wo Manabuhito no Tameni (Handbook of Social Work Practice with the Abused Children)* (pp. 154-172). Kyoto: Sekaishisosha.

Kamo, K., Oshita, Y., and Maeda, K. (2003). Jidouyougoshisetsu de Kurasu Higyakutaijido e no Koukateki na Shoguhou (Narrative Social Work for the Abused Child at Residential Care Institution for Children), *Studies of Social Work, 31 (2),* 47-53. Tokyo: Aikawashobo.

Kamo, K., and Oshita, Y. (2003). Naratibu Beisuto Medisun no Jissenrei (Narrative-Based Medicine from the Point of Medical Social Work), *Journal of Integrated Medicine, 13 (10),* 868-871. Tokyo: Igakushoin.

Kamo, K., and Oshita, Y. (2008). Ebidensu Beisuto Sosharuwaku no Tokushitsu 2 (Evidence Based Social Work 2), *Studies on Social Work, 34 (1),* 39-46. Tokyo: Aikawashobo.

Keeney, B. P. (1983). *Aesthetics of Change.* New York: The Guilford Press.

Laing, R. D. (1965). *The Divided Self: An Existential Study in Sanity and Madness.* London: Penguin Books.

Laird, J. (1985). Working with the Family in Child Welfare. In J. Laird and A. Hartman (eds.). *A Handbook of Child Welfare: Context, Knowledge, and Practice* (pp. 362-395). New York: Free Press.

Malcolm, N. (1994). Wittgenstein: A Religious Point of View? Ithaca, New York: Cornell University Press.

Nelson, T. S., and Thomas, F. N. (eds.). (2007). *Handbook of Solution-Focused Brief Therapy: Clinical Applications.* New York: The Haworth Press, Inc.

Miller, G. (1997). *Becoming Miracle Workers: Language Meaning in Brief Therapy.* New York: Walter de Gruyter, Inc.

Monette, D. R., Sullivan, T. J., and DeJomg, C. R. (2005). *Applied Social Research: A Tool for the Human Services.* Belmont: Brooks/Cole.

Oshita, Y. (2002). Sosharuwakujissen ni Okeru Shigen Shisutemu no Kouchiku 2: Jissenhen (Construction of the Resource System in Social Work Practice 2: A Case Analysis), *Japanese Journal of Social Welfare, 43 (1),* 44-53.

Oshita, Y. (2003). Nichijo-sei no Nakadeno Shigen (Resources in Life Worlds). In K. Kamo (ed.). *Nichijo-sei to Sosharu Waku (Life Worlds and Social Work Practice)* (pp. 83-112). Kyoto: Sekaishisosha.

Oshita, Y. (2003). Iryobamen niokeru Kaiketsushikou no Sosharu Waku (Solution Focused Health Care Social Work in Hospital Settings: Using the Social Construction Approach to Psychosomatic Disease), *Japanese Journal of Brief Psychotherapy*, 12, 12-25.

Oshita, Y. (2008). *Shienron no Genzai: Hoken Fukushi Ryoiki no Shiza kara. (New Human Services Theory).* Kyoto: Sekaishisosha.

Oshita, Y. (2008). Shakaikouseishugiteki Kouka Sokuteihou no Jissai. (Intervention Research Model Based on Social Constructionism). In K. Kamo and T. Nakaya (eds.). *Hyumansarbisu Chosahou wo Manabuhito no Tameni (A Handbook of Human Service Research)* (pp. 101-139). Kyoto: Sekaishisosha.

Oshita, Y. (2010). *Sapouto Nettowaku no Rinshoron. (Clinical Theory of Support Network)*. Kyoto: Sekaishisosha.

Oshita, Y., and Kamo, K. (2008). Shakaikouseishugiteki Kouka Sokutei Ron (Intervention Research Model Based on Social Constructionism). In K. Kamo and T. Nakaya (eds.). *Hyumansarbisu Chosahou wo Manabuhito no Tameni (A Handbook of Human Service Research)* (pp. 67-99). Kyoto: Sekaishisosha.

Parsons, T. (1951). *The Social System*. New York: Free Press.

Parsons, T., and Bales, R. F. (1955). *Family: Socialization and Interaction Process* (pp. 266-267). New York: The Free Press.

Pearce, W. B. (1994). *Interpersonal Communication: Making Social Worlds*. New York: Harper Collins College publishers, Inc.

Pearce, W. B. (2007). *Making Social Worlds: A Communication Perspective*. Oxford: Blackwell Publishing.

Sartre, J. P. (1965). *Nausea* (P. Baldick, Trans.). Harmondsworth: Penguin.

Theyer, B. A., and Wodarski, J. S. (eds.). (2007). *Social Work in Mental Health: An Evidence-Based Approach*. New Jersey: Willey and Sons.

Thomlison, B., and Thomlison, R. J. (1996). Behavior Theory and Social Work Treatment. In F. J. Turner (ed.). *Social Work Treatment: Interlocking Theoretical Approach (4th ed)*. New York: The Free Press.

Tomm, K. (1985). Circular Interviewing: A Multifaceted Clinical Tool. In D. Campbell and R. Draper (eds.). *Applications of Systemic Family Therapy: The Milan Approach* (pp. 33-45). New York: Grune and Stratton.

Tomm, K. (1987). Interventive Interviewing: Part 3. Reflexive questioning as a means to enable self-healing, *Family Process, 26,* 167-184.

Turner, J. H. (1991). *The Structure of Social Theory.* California: Wadsworth.

Watzlawick, P., Weakland, J., and Fisch, R. (1974). *Change: Principles of Problem Formation and Problem Resolution.* New York: W.W. Norton.

Watzlawick, P., Bavelas, J. B., and Jackson, D. (1967). *Pragmatics of Human Communication: A Study of Interactional Patterns, Pathologies, and Paradoxes.* New York: W. W. Norton.

Weeks, G. R., and L'Abate, L. (1982). *Paradoxical Psychotherapy: Theory and Practice with Individuals, Couples, and Families.* New York: Brunner/Mazel.

White, M., and Epston, D. (1990). *Narrative Means to Therapeutic Ends.* New York: W. W. Norton.

Wilden, A. (1980). *System and Structure: Eessays in Communication and Exchange 2nd ed.* London: Tavistock.

Wittgenstein, L. (1922). *Tractatus Logico-Philosophicus* (D. F. Pears and B. F. McGuinness, Trans.). London: Routledge and Kegan Paul Ltd.

Wittgenstein, L. (1999). *Tractatus Logico-Philosophicus* (C. K. Ogden, Trans.). New York: Dover Publications, Inc.

Wittgenstein, L. (1953). *Philosophical Investigations* (G. E. M. Anscombe, Trans.). Oxford: Basil Blackwell Ltd.

INDEX